By Faith
and a
Spin

To Shirley—
Bee
Blessed
Love,
Doris

The Story of Mech Apiaries

Doris Mech

ISBN 978-1-63885-711-2 (Paperback)
ISBN 978-1-63885-712-9 (Digital)

Covenant Books
11661 Hwy 707
Murrells Inlet, SC 29576
www.covenantbooks.com

To Grace and James Motherwell, my amazing computer genius grandchildren.

To Deena and Max Motherwell, Mary Simon, Carol Parlette, Marilyn Green, and Barbara Hampton who cheered me on.

To Paul, whose gentle wisdom guided me to focus on the positive.

And to my circle of Bible study fellowship friends, whose prayers brought this book to completion by the grace of God.

CONTENTS

ACKNOWLEDGMENTS

*M*ech Apiaries would never have existed if it had not been for so many wonderful generous families who gave us the privilege of putting beehives on their land. I list the following names now that I fondly remember. I know that my memory is not perfect, so please forgive me if I have omitted one or two. It was not intentional. The Knotts, the Donnelys, the Morgans, the Maranakas, the Masons, the Crosettas, the Wojewodskis, the Quackenbushes, the Ronbergers, the Baileks, the Uggins, the Beckwiths, the Kochevars, the Arhnkeils, the Davises, the Buffingtons, the Schusters, the Edgecombs, the Spaights, the Jelsmas, the Coopers, the Bussards, the Gudgers, the Kayleys, the Madges, the Jacobs, the Williams, the Bogans, the Winegerts, the Bensons, the Schillingers, the Johnsons, the Overlys, the Elliots, the Clarks, the Emericks, the Dykes, the Mastersons, the Frantzes, the Jakobsens, and Patches place.

PREFACE

*I*n the quiet early, early hours of morning, I was prompted to write the words "By Faith and a Spin" on a notebook near my bedside. That was six years ago. I was then caring for my husband, Don, who lived somewhere between the stages of dementia and Alzheimer's disease. I proceeded to write five pages to start the story.

Then between 2020 and 2021, the book was born, amidst the isolation of COVID-19.

Step-by-step, this book has evolved. The Lord has led me. The praise is to Him. "I will instruct thee and teach thee in the way which thou shalt go; I will guide thee with mine eye" (Psalm 32:8 KJV).

It is the story of Mech Apiaries, our family's livelihood and legacy.

In this modern world of smartphones, computers, and constantly changing technology, it is fascinating that one man, Donald R. Mech, was successfully able to step back in time and pursue a career in the ancient art of beekeeping. He learned to feel right at home in the apiary, like in a friendly welcoming neighborhood. Each group of beehives, called an apiary, was like a close-knit community. The bees cared for one another, using pheromones (their own scent signals). They mysteriously went about their work in orderly productive fashion, each doing their special tasks—the queen, the workers, and the drones. Don stepped into their world. It was his love and his passion.

CHAPTER 1

The Beginning, 1972

*M*ay 15, 1972, was an ordinary day in Renton, Washington, just outside of Seattle. Most of the fellows went to and fro to their jobs at the Boeing Company. Wives worked too but came home and prepared a tasty dinner so the family could come together to share their day's delights or dilemmas.

That was us. We were a typical family of three. Don, the Boeing engineer, pilot, mountain climber, and daddy. And me, Doris, his wife, part-time teacher, mother, junior choir director, cook, seamstress, and singer. How's that for a start? And there was Deena Marie, our sweet daughter, who just turned six a few weeks earlier.

When dinner was over and the last bite of homemade banana cream pie disappeared, it was time to settle into the evening activities. Deena loved playing with Felix, our Siamese cat; reading library books; or drawing. But her favorite was playing Sorry! with her daddy and me in front of a nice warm fire in the fireplace.

So as I cleaned up the kitchen, Don went to work, starting a cozy fire. Small kindling, logs, crumpled newspaper, *The Renton Record Chronicle.*

"Wait a minute, look at this newspaper article," he said. "It's about an old man who loved his job so much that he couldn't seem to retire. Can you imagine that? This is fascinating. Could a person really make a living like he did? He is an eighty-three-year-old beekeeper. Mac West. Maybe I should look into this. Who knows? I might like being my own boss for a change, setting my own goals and seeing a project completed from start to finish. Don't throw that paper away. I think I'll look into it one of these days."

And so the story began, the story of Mech Apiaries. That newspaper article sparked Don's interest in beekeeping as a profession. He was so excited with the whole idea, talking about it day and night as soon as he got home from his job at Boeing. There was a whole world of new knowledge to gain and explore.

He went to the downtown Seattle Public Library and was thrilled to find a large collection of books there on honeybees (*Apis mellifera,*) the apiary, and the beekeeping industry and its history. *The ABC and XYZ of Bee Culture, The Hive and the Honey-Bee,* and *American Honey Plants* were three of the first books he devoured. The more he read, the more he wanted to learn. He wanted to know if it was really possible to make a living like the old beekeeper in the newspaper. The seed had been planted.

We subscribed to two magazines: *American Bee Journal* and *Gleanings in Bee Culture.* They were totally fascinating.

A couple of months later, he pulled the newspaper story out of its safe resting place in the bottom dresser drawer and said, "Hey, Doris, I have an idea. Let's drive over to Mac West's house in Kent and see if he still has some honey for sale. Maybe he would be willing to talk to me. I'd really like to meet this guy. Some of his honey would be great in the sourdough bread we've been baking too!"

So off we went in our little red Volkswagen bug in search of the legendary eighty-three-year-old beekeeper.

We found his neat little wooden frame house on the east side of rural Kent. The "Honey for Sale" sign in his driveway was a dead giveaway that we were in the right place. But when we walked up to the porch, our excitement suddenly disappeared. We saw a homemade sign reading, "Sorry we missed you. Bee back soon." The beekeeper must have been off working with his bees. But there were a few jars of golden honey lined up on a shelf on his porch and a sign saying, "Two Dollars a Quart."

We slipped a two-dollar bill in the nearby jar and gladly toted a quart of his precious honey back home. We had a taste of Mac West's honey, but we had yet to meet this fascinating man.

Don couldn't wait. Within a matter of days, he was back on their front porch, this time gladly welcomed by the aged beekeeper and his cheerful wife, Myrtle. Mac was delighted to have a new "understudy" or "wannabee" as Myrtle would say.

They talked for over an hour. I wasn't there, but I heard all about it.

"To be a good beekeeper, you have to be dedicated to the bees. When the sun shines on a nice day, you can't go sailing, take a hike, or climb a mountain. The bees need you. You must care for them. You must know the condition of each hive, its queen, and its well-being. You'll learn the difference between the worker bee and a drone and the queen. I will teach you. I'll show you how I've lived with the bees and together how we have thrived over the last half a century. It's an amazing story, but are you sure you want to do this?"

"Yes, I'm sure," he replied.

"Okay then, there are a few things you'll need. A good sturdy pair of high-topped leather work boots. You gotta keep those bees from crawling up your pants. Sometimes they sting, you know! So here's an extra Mason Shoe catalog. I just happen to be a dealer. Here's something else you'll find interesting: a Walter T. Kelley catalog. They sell all kinds of things that beekeepers need. It's a whole new world. Take it home and look it over. But I always recommend making do with what you've got on hand. Be creative. Hey, how would you like to come along with me to the next beekeepers' meeting? We all learn a lot from each other. There's the Pierce County Beekeepers' Club that meets in Puyallup and the Puget Sound Beekeepers' Association that meets monthly in Seattle. John Stokes and I will pick you up. Okay? By the way, you'll be glad to meet John. He's a great beekeeper who is making woodenware these days in his own shop, frames and supers with grooved corners. He makes them to last too, handy things to know!"

"Sounds right up my alley," said Don. "I'm an independent guy who likes to do things right, my own way. I'll do the best I can. But I could sure learn a lot from you and John Stokes as well. I can see myself in an exciting role one day, with the honeybees. I'll be producing pure golden honey—special honey from the flowers that grow all around the Puget Sound. And yes, I'll even be able to make a living doing it! This will 'bee' totally fascinating. What a dream!"

So Don was hooked—hook, line and sinker as they say. Beekeeping was his new dream and passion. After a three months' leave of absence from Boeing, he decided to launch full-time into this new and challenging career. It was definitely a challenging step of faith. There would be no paycheck coming in like clockwork. We'd have to cut our expenses back and trust God for the future. Our limited savings would be used for the basics. But we would not need thousands of dollars invested in land, buildings, and expensive equipment right away, like other budding enterprises. We'd start small and work hard, trusting God's guiding hand. We'd do it by faith and a spin, a lot of hard work.

We could grow our own garden, maybe on our friend Norma's nice little blueberry farm. We'll get a Troy-Bilt. I could even till the ground. That would help our food bill. We could eat hamburgers instead of steak. We already had our closet full of clothes enough to last for years, and I had stacks of fabric to sew more clothes for Deena as she grew. We'd be getting lots of fresh air and exercise working with the bees, so we could skip mountain climbing and rock climbing. We could go camping with the bees.

It would be hard to give up our flying and gliding, but we'd choose to watch the bees do that. Another major expense we had to prayerfully consider was healthcare. Since we were all young and healthy, we decided to opt out of health insurance and trust in God alone to meet our needs.

We would need a pickup truck and later a flatbed. The Volkswagen bug wouldn't quite do it. Then, of course, we'd need the wooden beehives. Don could build those in the nice big workshop in our basement. We heard about a place to get free scrap wood, a Boeing industrial dump on top of a hill that is now the beautiful New Castle golf course.

Don worked nonstop, meticulously measuring, sawing, glueing, pounding in nails, and then painting. By springtime, he'd built twenty deep boxes called supers, five covers, five bottom boards, and five pallets. In each super, there were ten frames with beeswax sheets of foundation. Those we ordered, ready to be assembled, from the Walter T. Kelley Company in Clarkson, Kentucky. Now our rec room was stacked to the brim with enough equipment for five beehives. However, one thing was missing: the bees. But not for long.

They were on their way from the beekeepers in the Sacramento Valley. And so it was, on a very early morning in April 1973, that our telephone rang persistently off the wall until we sleepily stumbled down the hall and into the kitchen to answer it.

"Hello. Are you the Mechs? Your bees are here, in the post office. Come get 'em *now*! Gloria is allergic to beestings."

"Okay, we'll be there in a few minutes."

It was only three blocks to the post office, so Don excitedly put on his new white coveralls and his high-topped Mason farm boots. With a hive tool, smoker, veil, and gloves in hand, he hopped into the pickup truck to get our first honeybees. It never even dawned on him to have his morning coffee and sourdough pancakes.

The packaged bees made the trip from California very well. They came in screen wire crates with the queens in separate little containers. The postal workers breathed a sigh of relief when he came to get them. And Don was off on his dream come true: being a beekeeper.

Don had carefully prepared for this day. The pristine, beautifully handcrafted white beehives were already situated in Norma Knott's blueberry farm. The hives were located near the western edge of her property on a slight hill where they would get the first rays of morning sunshine.

Getting the new bees into the hives went as planned, just like the book said. Walter T. Kelley's classic book, *How to Keep Bees and Sell Honey*, was perfect for a novice, first-time beekeeper. Don had read the instructions so many times that they were clearly in his head.

There were many firsts for us to experience, like the first time to observe how quickly the bees oriented themselves into their new location. They were almost immediately at work, buzzing into the flowers on the blueberry farm and beyond. We sat on the grass in amazement, watching as first they flew in little circles back and forth, memorizing landmarks and then finally flying away to bring back home the sweet nectar and pollen to their own hive.

There was no question about which hive was home. They made a beeline right into their own white pristine new home. It was beautiful to watch. Our first bees started out with fresh new sheets of beeswax foundation. So their first job, before anything else, was to build up the comb with beeswax. This they did in a matter of days. The worker bees all worked together in amazing unity.

When we opened up the hives a few days later, we saw the fruit of their labor; a beautiful honeycomb was drawn out deeply, and in the bottom of each cell lay a tiny egg. The queen bee was doing her job, just like it said in the book. Around the edges on the outer combs, there was even some golden nectar and pollen. The aroma was delightful. I remember it to this very day: the perfume of sweet nectar and beeswax. The bees would need all the honey they were producing to build up their colonies. It was such a temptation to pull some of the new treasured honey. But we heeded the advice of our sage mentor, Mac West: "First, let the bees fill up two boxes"—deep supers—"then later add another super for honey for you to harvest!"

So we treated the bees gently, with great respect and tender care, using just a small puff of smoke from the smoker to scatter the workers away from the frames we needed to handle and inspect. We were mindful to use gentle slow movements, being careful to never drop or bang a frame back into position. The bees were our new partners, but could they actually be built up to supply the basic needs of our family?

They were so tiny, but what amazing creatures of God's handiwork and design. I remember the first time Don showed us a frame covered with the bees.

"Look," he said, "do you see the queen bee? She's about twice as long as the others. She is surrounded by about a half-dozen worker bees who are taking good care of her. They feed her and groom her as she goes about her task of egg laying. She can lay two thousand eggs in a single day! She can even decide to lay a fertilized egg, which will develop into a female worker bee or an unfertilized egg which will grow into a drone," the boy bees. "It's all so amazing, isn't it? I read there's been more written about honeybees than any other subject, with only one exception, and that's the Holy Bible."

So now we were convinced that this would be our new career. The crucial deciding factor and question had been solved: neither one of us developed an allergic reaction to the occasional sting which is something every beekeeper must be mindful of.

The first beautiful white hives were made out of salvaged materials, but now it was time to move forward into serious production. That would require lots of lumber and a truck to haul it.

We found a used flatbed, one-ton Chevy that we nicknamed Galloping Gertie. It wasn't fancy, but it did its job—usually. We paid a thousand dollars' cash—never once using credit. In fact, to Don's dying day, he never owned a credit card.

Walt Stickel drove with him to Western Bee Supply in Montana and came back with lumber stacked high in the flatbed, tied down with ropes using a nifty trucker's knot that Walt demonstrated. Walt was also a new beekeeper. They were soon the best of friends. We were able to store the lumber in Taylor's barn in nearby New Castle in trade for anticipated honey. The truck was also parked off the street—a block away from our home in the Renton Highlands, on a side lot of Mary Gwin's property. She too graciously awaited some sweet honey in return.

Don began the giant task of building all the equipment for the beehives in our basement workshop. He worked with the precision of his electrical engineer training, a perfectionist, down to the last detail. His goal was to build equipment for eighty more hives by the following spring.

In the meantime, I taught sewing classes for Green River Community College. In addition, I did sewing and alterations for a local cleaners' shop as well as some tailoring and dressmaking for private customers. I even took a stint at being a Welcome Wagon hostess for the city of Renton, a job I truly enjoyed.

Don continued to work hard building up all the equipment and laying the groundwork for our new venture while I tried to bring in cash for our daily necessities. We had a goal. With God's help, we chose to get to work, like the saying goes, "putting our noses to the grindstone." This meant we'd have to forget about many little luxuries and frills, like having T-Bone steaks twice a week. But the hamburger was good. We never went hungry. We were greatly thankful for all the wild huckleberries and wild blackberries in our freezer. Pies made from the berries were a celebration indeed. In addition, homemade bread and cookies continued to give our kitchen a welcome aroma. The Boeing paycheck did not come in anymore, but God was leading us on our new pathway. We'd trust in him to lead us day by day. Surely, his guiding hand would orchestrate our future. I wore a big pin on my lapel those days. It said, "I Believe in Miracles."

The Call

How could a man so strong and tall
Set his eyes on a goal so strange to all?
Forsaking the pathway of study he'd trod,
Then say "goodbye" to his Boeing job!
Goodbye to that biweekly check.
Goodbye to being one spoke in a wheel!
To most it seems strange,
But to Don it was real—
Real adventure indeed!
Producing honey with honeybees!

So could it be, on an evening fair,
As smoke curled up in the chimney there,
God's plan was coming into view.
His voice was real,
He'd see us through.
He'd lead us gently day by day.
The call was ours.
Would we obey?
Could we by faith learn something new
And be sustained by what bees do?

January 6, 2020

CHAPTER 2

Under the Shadow of the Almighty

November 1, 1973

3311 Northeast Eleventh Place
Renton, Washington
98055

Dear Aunt Lena and Uncle Luis,

We were glad to get your letter last month.
No, we have not moved yet. We have not decided
on any one location. Montana is only one possi-

bility. We want a farm with five or ten acres with a three- or four-bedroom house on it and another good building that could be made into a honey house.

We have lots of good honey to sell. We got about five hundred pounds from our five colonies of bees this past summer. We are selling it mostly retail, some bartering too. It's fireweed honey. We took our bees up in the mountains and left them there this summer. We got a permit to leave them on a state-owned land.

I am teaching one sewing class at Green River Community College. Yesterday, I signed up for substitute teaching in Renton. This morning at six thirty, the phone rang, and I was called to substitute for the choir director at Renton High School. How's that for a quick reply?

I thank the Lord because I'd been trying to find some other work. I didn't realize I could get a certificate for substituting until only yesterday. And here I am in the classroom today!

Don is busy being a carpenter these days. He's happy setting his own pace and seeing all the boxes stack up. Our basement looks like a factory now. Next spring, he plans to drive down to California and bring back around eighty packages of bees on the back of our pickup. Our garden is nearly gone, but we sure enjoyed it a lot. That Troy-Bilt rototiller Don decided to purchase was worth its weight in gold. Yes, gold potatoes, bush beans, tomatoes, lettuce, cabbage, beets, parsley, carrots, radishes, and zucchini.

The zucchini produced the best for us. We ate it in every way imaginable, and I even froze some. One of our favorites was zucchini bread with honey in it. Oh yes, there were green onions and rutabagas too. It surely pays to have a garden. We had our garden at our friend Norma's house where the beehives were last spring.

Love,
Doris, Don, and Deena

In 1973, the bees produced five hundred pounds of honey. Our small apiary of three hives had expanded into five colonies with the addition of two swarms we rescued. Now we had to find a place to extract the "slidey," the sticky honey from the combs. And I *definitely* did *not* want it happening in my *kitchen*. No sticky floors in my house.

So one Sunday morning, Don asked me to ride along with him in search of someone who might appreciate honeybees and honey. We needed to find a place to extract all that honey that was still on the hives in the mountains, and then we also needed a good place to locate those five hives for the winter. I agreed to join him on a searching journey of faith that Sunday after attending customary worship services at our church.

We were led to a little farm on the outskirts of Renton Highlands.

"I think this is the place," I said as we slowly pulled up the driveway. "Why don't you go up to the house and talk to the people who live here. I'll stay in the car and pray."

That was the day we met Henry and LaVonne Morgan.

As my prayers ascended heavenward, I was reminded of the words Pastor Walter Luttman had recently spoken in one of his timely sermons, "When the Lord smiles on us" and "There's no such thing as good luck," at our little church, Bethlehem Lutheran.

As a child, my mother had taught me to know the Lord. She had instilled in me the awe and love of the Savior. Before my third birthday, the words of the beloved shepherd's psalm, Psalm 23, were tucked away in my memory so that my heart was overwhelmed with joy as I realized that, yes, God was truly leading us and smiling down upon us.

Meeting Henry and LaVonne Morgan was a delightful double blessing. They loved and appreciated the value of honeybees. They welcomed us with open arms. Before we left their farm that Sunday afternoon, we'd had a fun tour of their gardens, orchard, and barns and heard all about their amazing family. We also had exactly what we needed with the next step of our budding beekeeping business.

We had a perfect place to bring our hives for the winter and an unused outbuilding where we could extract the honey. Wow! In exchange for these things, they eagerly agreed to a barter deal of sweet golden honey. This was truly a miracle.

The bees were still in the mountains near Mount Rainier. Together, Don and his avid beekeeping friend Walt Stickel moved them to their wintering grounds. There was no electronic boom then to lift those heavy hives. Together they manually got the hives up onto the flatbed using a hand truck and rolling each hive up a plank. It took lots of young manpower. They figured there was a half-ton load combining Walt's hives with ours. The hives were brimming with precious fireweed honey.

So what were we going to call our honey? We needed a name on the label. Funny, we hadn't even thought of that. Should it be Golden Glow pure honey or Pooh Bear's Best? Or how about Eden's Delight? The choice, of course, was ours alone. We decided on something totally unique and rather mysterious. Our brand label would be Mech Apiaries. We do have a rare name. There are not very many Mechs in the USA. An apiary, by definition, is a place where honeybees are kept. So Mech Apiaries was born. We drove into Downtown Seattle and made it official, getting our business license.

Now we were ready to purchase jars and lids at wholesale prices. The good folks at NW Glass were so understanding and helpful. They kindly directed us just where to go as we backed up very carefully between huge commercial rigs at the loading dock. We bought as many jars as we could fit on the back of our little pickup. Then after carefully tying down the load, we drove away on the freeway to our friends' house—Tim and Ginny Schlitzer. They had graciously agreed to let us use their vacant bedroom for storage, in exchange for honey, of course.

More and more people were eagerly anticipating our first vintage crop of golden honey. One more thing, however, was essential— an extractor. We found a used two-frame reversible model from a beekeeper in the Yakima Valley. It was a simple machine with a handle that, when cranked by hand, literally spun the honey to the edge of the metal tank. There was a gate on the bottom edge that, when opened, allowed the honey to drain into a five-gallon bucket.

We had a big sieve that just fit on top of the bucket to strain out any bits of wax or other debris. But even before the frames of honeycomb were placed into the extractor, the wax needed to be cut off. Just to the left of the extractor, Don built a stand for a round metal tub. Yes, it was my old bathtub as a small child. Anyway, Don fixed it up as an uncapping tank, with an electrically heated big knife to carefully cut the wax away from both sides of each comb. Then the frames could be put in the extractor to spin the honey out. Every bit of wax was precious. We saved it all, packing it into five-gallon buckets that we got free from Jack in the Box up the street.

We never could figure out how to make those buckets stop smelling like dill pickles, so we did have to go out and purchase new ones for the honey, but for the uncapping wax, it worked fine. On the opposite end of this extracting room was a little woodburning camp stove that did a great job of heating up the air temperature to eighty-five or ninety degrees. This warmed the honey which was stacked in the supers all the way to the ceiling. Talk about a sweet shop. All Don wore for this job were shorts, a white canvas apron, and a white cap on his head. It was such hard work cutting the wax off the honeycomb and spinning all the honey out. But he was in his glory. At the end of each day, he carried the golden sweet treasure in five-gallon buckets into the pickup, drove home, and then carried the buckets, two at a time, back into our house and down the stairs to our rec room. Each bucket weighed about sixty pounds. Then he lifted them up and very slowly poured them into the big bottling tank through a strainer covered with cheesecloth.

Our whole house smelled like sweet honey; it was marvelous. It more than made up for the fact that our rec room now looked like a factory. When all was said and done, we had about five hundred pounds of fireweed honey. The very first jar went as a token of appreciation to a man we highly revered, Hegge Iverson, the founder of Burden Bearers—a Christian counseling organization in Seattle. Then the payback barters began. A quart here and a gallon there. Norma Knott, Mary Gwin, Leo Healeys, the Morgans, Tim and Ginny Schlitzer, Gerhard Mueller, to name a few. We even bartered for babysitting and a dozen eggs. Everyone loved that incredible fireweed honey. We bottled up several cases for retail sales from our house. Good news spread fast; Mech Apiaries has the best honey ever.

The following list is a partial ledger of folks who came to our house in the Renton Highlands in 1973. Note that food was taxed that year.

Mike Poulous
Linda McElroy, 3 pounds, $2.25
Jon Zack, 1 pound, $1.00
Jan Vanera, 11 1/2 ounces, $0.84
Judy and Larry Gibson, 11 1/2 ounces, $0.84
Winona Richardson, 11 1/2 ounces, $0.84
Sharon Moore, 11 1/2 ounces, $0.84
Mike and Marlene Wills, 2 pounds, $1.90
Edwin and Anna Dietrich, 11 1/2 ounces, $0.84
Clara and Roy, 1 gallon, $9.48
Chuck Luttman, 1 gallon, $9.48
Ralph Drew, 2 pounds, $2.00
Geneva Sargent, 1 pound, $1.00
Sharon Thompson, 2 pounds, $1.90
Chet and Yvonne Goad, 11 1/2 ounces, $.084
Pastor Eggers, 11 1/2 ounces, $0.84
Bernice Koester, 10 pounds, $10.00
June Stultz, 2 pounds, $2.00
Laura Cowan, 2 pounds, $2.00
Mr. Malmanato, 11 1/2 ounces, $0.84
Barbara Gary, 1 gallon, $9.48
Will and Erica Heisinger, 1 gallon, $9.48

Maynard and Rose Svor, 2 pounds, $2.00
Dick and Ellen Taylor, 1 pound, $1.00
Ernest Pearson, 1 gallon, $9.48
Marilyn Green, 2 pounds, $2.00
Lynn Hampton, 2 pounds, $2.00
Deryl Hampton, 2 pounds, $2.00
Ralph Kivett, 2 pounds, $2.00

CHAPTER 3

By Faith

"*W*hen Satan appears to stop our path and fills us with fears, we'll triumph by faith; he cannot take from us," though oft he had tried. "This heart-cheering promise, the Lord will provide."

In the beginning of our new venture, we had determined to walk by faith, trusting in the Lord to provide for all our needs. So far, everything had gone very well. We were each young and healthy, and God had spared us from any unexpected mishaps.

Our frugal little nest egg of savings was slowly going into all the costs of building up a beekeeping enterprise. We were so happy to have a priceless pure product that people everywhere very highly treasured.

It seemed, at that point, that we could eventually actually make a living selling honey right from our door, if we continued working hard and building up our hive count. Five beehives had produced about five hundred pounds of honey. So Don set himself a goal of building eighty more colonies for next year. He went to work in the woodworking shop off the rec room in our basement, like an eager beaver.

Hive boxes or supers were stacked everywhere in the lower level of our home. We put up a "Honey for Sale" sign, and people began coming right to our door. I continued to daily surprise Don with new recipes I developed upstairs in our kitchen, *all* with a touch of honey, of course!

I saved us lots of money using my home economics skills—sewing and cooking. I made most of Deena's clothes, as she continued to grow out of smaller sizes. That was no problem at all because, after all, I'd been a sewing instructor a few years ago. I also made gifts for family and friends at Christmastime instead of shopping at the mall. And like I said before, we gave up our expensive hobbies. It was "*all* for the bees—for the glory of God."

Trust in the Lord and let him be the Good Shepherd. This, of course, means to actually take the Bible off the shelf to read it and to do what it says, listening to the still, small voice of the Holy Spirit, who promises to be our counselor and guide. It all sounds good and easy. But easy it was not. There were bound to be roadblocks and detours along the way.

A major trial came late in 1973 when I discovered a lump in my breast. Determined to trust in God, I was given hope by a scripture I found in Psalms 42 and 43. And it was repeated three times on the same page: "Hope thou in God. For I shall yet praise Him, who is the health of my countenance and my God" (Psalms 43:5 KJV). This was very comforting to me, but I also needed to find a doctor and get checked out.

That could be very expensive and wipe us out financially. I prayed, and so did my close circle of praying friends. Somehow, I ended up at the Glasier Clinic in Seattle with an excellent low-cost care. The lump ended up just being a cyst which was drained and never gave me any further problems. What a blessing. For several weeks after that, I remember wearing a pin that said PTL—praise the Lord.

CHAPTER 4

1974, Expansion

This was a year of expansion. We went from five beehives to *eighty-five*, building it all up by hand. In January, Don placed an order of eighty packaged bees with a beekeeper in the Sacramento Valley. We drove all the way to California to pick them up in our Mazda truck.

He had tied down hooks welded to the exact needed spots on the truck. No detail was spared. This beeman would just do it. We'd bring all those bees to Washington, and there would soon be not only one apiary but many—Mech Apiaries. We were living our dream.

Now it was time to search for more locations on which to keep the bees. Mac West, our trusted mentor, was a great help. "Look for a location where bees will get the morning sun, not too close to peoples' clotheslines and obviously where there are good honey plants growing—gardens, flowering trees, wild blackberry bushes, etc. People with pretty flowers and gardens usually appreciate and value honeybees. Look for a lot of dandelions as well. Dandelions have a lot of pollen."

So off we went again on a search for apiary sites—with a prayer as always for the Lord's guidance. We wanted to have our new apiaries nearby where we could manage them and build them up into strong hives ready for honey production by June. We were welcomed with our beehives to the properties of more gracious people: the Masons, the Donnelys, and the Healeys. All these folks were happy to have sweet honey bartered in exchange for keeping the bees on their land.

The woodenware was all built and painted for eighty more colonies of bees. It was all stacked up in our basement. We'd found "beeyards," as Don used to say. We had the bees ordered.

Now we waited for a telephone call from Horvath's Bee Farm in Sheridan, California. They had given their good word to call us a couple of days before our order would be ready. The determining factor that came into play was the weather. A rainy spell could mean delay because the queen bees needed nice weather to go on their mating flights and to be ready for production once they were placed in our hives.

The phone rang one morning as expected. "Hello, your bees should be ready to pick up in three days."

"Hooray! Great. We'll be there to pick them up. See you then."

That day, while I packed our bags, Don set out our brand-new hives on the Mason and Donnely properties. There were a few cows in the Mason's field, so I remember he put up an electric fence around the apiary just to avoid any unwanted emergencies.

We drove as far as Forest Grove and dropped Deena Marie off for a visit with my parents—her dearly beloved grandma and grandpa.

Then we drove on to Cottage Grove for dinner with my aunt Rosetta and uncle Earl. It was a nice time around their table but too short a visit because we wanted to drive across the Oregon-California border before finding a motel. It was raining when we awakened in Marysville the next morning.

Steady rain. We had arranged to stay with my aunt Elsie and Uncle Earl in Auburn. They graciously put us up in their camper trailer in the backyard. We heard the rain pounding down all night long. When we called the beekeepers the next morning, our suspicions were true—there would be a delay in our bee order. We were blessed to have a good long visit with my dear aunt Elsie and uncle Earl. I still treasure some of the handmade linens that she gave me in 1974, as she shared stories of her past. We were there several days, waiting for the weather to clear.

Then one evening as we were eating dinner together, the phone on the wall rang. Someone was looking for us. Were we there? Yes. The news was sad and very unexpected. Uncle Earl, whom we had visited only days ago in Cottage Grove, had died of a massive heart attack.

Could I please hurry home to be with the family and attend the funeral? Our family had always been very close and supportive of one another, but this time, I had to say no to my family. My heart ached to let them down, but Don and I had a higher calling now, and it was to take care of honeybees and establish Mech Apiaries, standing by my husband's side as a helpmate.

Obviously, the sun did come out again as it always does. We got our eighty packages of bees—ten for Walt at three pounds per package—and twelve extra queens. There were no extra stops along the way back home to Renton. We took turns driving and arrived back home very sleepy eyed from our 1,626-mile round trip marathon. We examined our precious cargo.

In the darkness of night, we heard no buzzing sound at all. We shined a flashlight beam into a couple of the packages. They were not even moving. Were they even alive? Had they survived the long open-air ride from California? Suddenly, we were worried. They must have gotten too chilled. So we decided right then and there to unload them all off the truck and carry them down the stairs to our basement.

It was definitely warmer in the house. Job done. Then we fell into bed exhausted. Exhausted but yet exhilarated. The bees were in our house.

In the morning, it was quite a different story. They were very much alive. Alive and buzzing. Eighty packages of bees in our basement—all alive and buzzing. We carefully brushed a little sugar water on the screens of the packages to give the bees a refreshing drink. Then we loaded up half of them, forty packages, ready to go to their new homes on the Mason Farm.

Mac West was there that morning, teaching Don exactly how to do it. After doing it forty times, with Mac's help, he was confident and competent to take on the task himself in the Donnely yard.

According to Mac West, the new packaged bees should be built up and strong, ready to produce a good crop of honey for us in a couple of months. He encouraged us to look ahead with a plan as to where the bees should be located to make the most honey. Mac had learned the tricks of the trade as a master beekeeper over the years, winning many blue ribbons for the highly prized honeys of the greater Puget Sound region: Mount Rainier fireweed, huckleberry, blackberry, raspberry, maple blossom, and snowberry.

Mac advised us to truck the bees over to Harstine Island where they could gather nectar from the wild evergreen huckleberries. We'd never been to that island, but Mac volunteered to show us exactly where to go and introduced Don to key people who were happy to welcome the beehives.

We met Francis Madge and her goose. Francis lived close to an old pioneer cemetery and just down the road from the oyster beds. Don set up his tent on her property to work with the bees.

We also met the Winegerters—wonderful, gracious people on the island. The Winegerters' farm was on the central part of the island—a charming rural property in a picturesque setting. They were the nicest people you could ever hope to meet, and they took a real liking to Deena. They gave our city girl a real taste of the country—a fertilized chicken egg. We put it in a little incubator and excitedly watched it hatch into a baby chick.

Most importantly, on Harstine Island, the bees made a marvelous crop of huckleberry honey. What a delight that was! We had been so thrilled with the fireweed honey made last summer near Mount Rainier. The fireweed honey was very light and clear and so delicious, but the huckleberry honey almost tasted like butterscotch candy. It was more amber in color and had the most marvelous aroma as Don extracted it in Morgan's little honey house.

When the bees no longer had nectar coming in from the wild evergreen huckleberry bushes on Harstine Island, it was time to immediately truck them to a new area that was now brimming with nectar from other sources. In July, we could count on the wild blackberries to be in bloom in the verdant lowlands of the Puget Sound.

The wild blackberries seemed to be growing everywhere, even in the vacant city lots. The honeybees flew right to those blossoms to sip the sweet nectar and, in the process, also gathered the pollen making pollination occur, thus producing all those tasty blackberries. But to us, the goal was to capture the sweet fruity nectar that our bees would transform into another marvelous variety of honey.

After removing the supers of huckleberry honey, we wasted no time and loaded the beehives up the plank and onto the flat bed of Galloping Gertie. We took them back to the Mason and Donnely yards on the outskirts of Renton, and they went to work that month making blackberry honey. Around the end of July, the blackberry honey flow ceased, so we removed the fresh honey from the hives, making sure each frame was capped over with wax. The covering ensured that the honey was "cured" and would not ferment from too much moisture. However, some were eager to try making some mead from the fermented honey—but that's another story.

We were soon getting more honey than we knew what to do with. It was time to increase our circle of happy customers.

"I know," said Don. "Let's park our Galloping Gertie truck by a well-traveled road where passersby can see it. I'll make a big sign:

'Honey for Sale.' You can pack a picnic lunch, and we'll see how many people will stop and buy a jar or two."

Long story short, that day was not a success. We had very few customers.

"There is still a lot of honey to sell!" I said. "I know what. Let's go down to Pike Place Market in Seattle. That's such a fun place. I'm sure we'd be able to sell a lot more there with all the other farmers. Maybe they'd let us have a table to set out our honey."

The next day, I dialed the telephone number of Pike Place Market and spoke with the market master.

"Yes, we are looking for more farmers. Would you like to come next Saturday?" he said. "Just be here at seven a.m., and I'll show you where to set up your display. I'll give you an eight-foot table. The fee will be fifty cents to rent that space for the day. We look forward to seeing you. Honey is a wonderful farm crop. You'll be welcomed here."

That was in the middle of July 1974, our spot in history as a farmer at the world-famous Pike Place Market in Seattle, Washington, had begun—a legacy that would last for forty years.

That first day, we loaded up our Volkswagen bug to the brim with jars of huckleberry and blackberry honey packed in quart-sized and one-pound glass jars and a few five-pound shiny metal tins. We only had a half-dozen little jars of the fireweed from 1973, but we brought that too. We set up our display on gold-colored placemats, and Deena proudly held up the sign I had made: "Organic Honey." Don wore the button we were given that very first day. We were the sixty-first farmer to come that year, and I still have the historic button. They gave me number 61 on that unforgettable day. We saw so many people streaming by. It actually made me dizzy. A sea of humanity moving by right before our eyes—all potential honey customers. The challenge was to catch their attention and make a personal contact.

Before the day was over, we purchased a box of toothpicks and began giving away little tastes of our honey. Once people tasted it, very often, they wanted more to take home. We sold jar after jar that day and went back home with a much lighter load in our Volkswagen.

It sure was a better way to bring our golden harvest to the public than selling by the side of the road.

Life was getting busier and more interesting day by day. We felt confident that the Lord was guiding our lives. Mac West kept in touch with Don nearly every day. When the phone rang, it never took him very long to bolt up the stairs from his woodworking shop in the basement to answer it. "Hey, Don. It's time to get those bees of yours up to the mountains. I hear the fireweed flowers are dripping with nectar! There's no time to waste. If the bees are not there, then all that good nectar will just fall on the ground. What a waste that would be!" When Mac West spoke, Don moved into action. He greatly admired this seasoned old beekeeper and was grateful for his advice.

Together with Walt Stickel, Don moved all the beehives up to the foothills of Mount Rainier. Fireweed flowers covered the logged-off mountains with a beautiful rosy hue. Don got two permits: one from the US Forest Service and the other from the Department of Natural Resources, Washington State. Don and Walt put up electric fences around both of these apiaries because there were definitely bears in the area. And it was no secret—Winnie the Pooh did *love* honey. Don didn't want to take any chances of bears getting into our beehives. He went the extra mile and wired cans of cat food to the fencing so the hungry bear would get a big surprise shock right on the tongue when he came near. This worked too. It was evident by the pile of bear droppings right on the spot that he had decided to leave in a big hurry and feast on wild berries in the forest instead or maybe a fish in the nearby mountain streams. We kept the bears out of our hives that year.

The big toads were a different story. There was really no way we could figure out how to stop them from coming right up to the entrance of the hives and eating the bees. Their tongues must have been at least six inches long. Of course, when we happened to be up in the mountains that day, as evening approached, we could shoo them away. But we had a lot of other important things to do at home. We couldn't be with the bees every day.

When Deena and I came along, it was a real treat. We brought watermelon and hid it away in a nearby icy cold mountain stream. A couple of times, we brought our tent and a little kerosene cookstove and stayed overnight under all the beautiful stars—memories I will never forget. We even heard sounds of the wild elks bugling, coyotes howling, and nighthawks making eerie sounds swooping through the darkening sky. And occasionally when the wind was just right, the air was filled with the most heavenly sweet aroma from the fireweed honey the busy worker bees were processing. It was a wonder that every bear on the mountain didn't come and help themselves. But fortunately, we were so blessed with a nice crop of fireweed honey in 1974. In fact, it was such an abundant amount of honey that we began selling it to our first wholesale accounts.

1974 gross sales:

wholesale
Honey Dew Nursery, $30.00
Curt Hutchinson, $76.70
Carlson Brothers, $444.30
Covey's Market, $48.42
Farmer's Market, $19.92
total: $619.34

retail sales (Taxed honey—yes, it was taxed in 1974.):
first quarter, $80.43
second quarter, $36.33
third quarter, $206.91
fourth quarter, $290.51
total: $614.18

Plus, over two hundred pounds of honey barters for everything you can imagine:

storage place for empty jars
storage place for lumber

rent for land to put bees on
rent for land to garden
rent to use outbuilding for honey house
manure for the garden
fresh eggs
haircut
babysitting
sharing the ride
chiropractor

When 1974 was said and done, we had harvested over two thousand pounds of honey from the blackberry, huckleberry, fireweed, and mountain flowers. And after holiday sales, it was nearly sold out. We looked forward to the following spring, when the bees would go to work for us again.

Don decided to split all the stronger hives come spring, so he was busy building more equipment to house our expanding apiary operation. He also decided to build an observation hive so we could bring live bees with us when we sold our honey.

That was definitely an excellent idea. It drew people of all ages into our display so we could talk with them. What a joy that was. We had a fascinating gift to share with the world—the awesome honeybees themselves and the incredible offering of their harvest that we were blessed to share, sweet golden honey, extracted and in the comb.

Chapter 5

One Day in 1975

I heard about Wendle, as I'll call him, on the day my beekeeping husband Don returned from a long day of caring for his honeybees located up in the foothills of the Olympic Mountains. It had been a long day, up at the first crack of dawn. With a hearty breakfast of sourdough pancakes, hot coffee, and grapefruit smothered in Mount Rainier fireweed honey, he was off. Off down the freeway, headed in the opposite direction of most folks on their way to city jobs. He was headed to the hills, where thirty colonies of honeybees busily went about their ancient task of making honey. They were on Mackie Timberland, on logged-off slopes, ablaze with pink fireweed flowers in full bloom. The beehives were all lined up in perfectly straight rows on a landing just off the logging road. An electric fence circled all thirty of them to discourage any hungry bears.

He got out of his truck and lit his smoker, ready to inspect each hive. As he scanned the peaceful, quiet mountainside, he noticed something quite unusual: animal tracks of something he'd never seen in the wild before. They were definitely *not* deer or elk tracks. They were bigger. What in the world had been walking around the apiary, twenty miles away from the nearest town? Well, all the beehives looked okay. That was a relief, he thought.

He went about his work. Work he loved. Tending his bees in the fresh mountain air. Suddenly, he noticed something unusual— something was moving in his direction just down the mountain to his left. He couldn't quite make it out. What in the world was he seeing? No, it couldn't be, not way up here in the mountains. But here they were, a man and his cow. *So those must be cow tracks on the ground*, he thought.

The man, Wendle, whose big cowboy hat shaded his shaggy beard, held in his hand a rope. On the other end of the rope was his cow following slowly along. He stopped to talk. Wendle was an interesting fellow.

"A bit strange maybe," said Don. "He's living in the woods, looking for gold and minerals. But he seemed nice enough. He said he'd be watching out for our bees, and he'd sure love a little honey to eat. I said, 'Maybe we could work something out like a trade or barter.' Then Wendle reached into his pocket and pulled out a shiny piece of rock that sparkled like crystal. He gave it to me and said, 'I'll give you another piece if you give me some honeycomb next time. That's so special. It's worth its weight in gold.'"

"Got a deal," said Don. And they shook hands in a gentlemen's agreement.

"Stop by and see me on your way out," he said. "I'll show you what I'm doing up in these hills. I'm just down the road under those three tall cedar trees you can see in the distance."

Don did just that. He stopped to talk to Wendle on his way back down the mountain. He saw his deep firepit where he melted down the rock. He saw his dwelling—similar looking to an Indian teepee but constructed out of thin planks of cedar. A nearby stream furnished clear sparkling water, and just a short distance down the hill was a corral where his cow was.

"How would you and Deena like to come with me and meet Wendle next time I go to that apiary? We could have a picnic after I do my work in the beeyard. We could even bring a watermelon and chill it in the icy mountain stream just above the apiary. You two could go for a little walk in the woods. It's really beautiful up there."

"Okay, let's do it," I said.

So the following week, all three of us headed out to the Olympics in our Mazda pickup fully loaded with supplies for the bees and our picnic lunch, including that anticipated cold watermelon. We didn't see Wendle that day. He was probably out looking for gold or gemstones, but we had an unforgettable day. Seeing Wendle's campsite was just the beginning. First of all, Don led the way to the icy cold mountain stream. It was just a short distance up the hill, on the edge of a deep forest. We paused for a breath and heard the gentle trickling of water flowing down the mountainside. Then we descended into a ravine and realized the air temperature was at least ten degrees cooler down there where the creek flowed. The water itself was icy cold. We found a spot behind a rock to stash our watermelon. It would be so nice and cold when we were ready for lunch.

Back at the apiary, Don said, "I have a couple of hours of work to do with the bees. You two can go for a hike. Just don't get lost. We'll have our lunch when you get back. Just blow your whistle if you can't find the apiary, and I'll blow my whistle in return. Have fun."

Deena and I were off, on our way with our hiking boots on and day packs with fresh water and snacks. We walked down the hillside through big stumps of cedar surrounded by four- or five-feet tall fireweed flowers. We walked through a gorge with cliffs of sparkly crystal towering on our left. We wondered if we would see Wendle. The only tracks that we saw on the ground, however, were those of deer or elk.

To the right, we saw a small stand of deciduous trees with white bark and a pond nearby.

"Oh, doesn't that look pretty down there?" I said. "Let's go check it out."

"Okay, here I come," said Deena.

We walked past a pond and got a glimpse of a frog jumping off a mossy log into the water. We saw where a beaver had made a dam. Then we spotted a red huckleberry bush loaded with ripe berries—so ripe you could just smell their sweetness. We stopped and had our fill of delicious berries.

On we walked through a dark forest of cedar with ferns and moss covering the ground below the trees. It was magically lovely. We lost track of time, absorbed in the beauty of nature, admiring every plant and mushroom and every snail and slug. Soon it was time to head back.

"Let's sit down on that nice log and have our snack before we head back," I said.

We refreshed ourselves with fruit leather, Triscuits, and cheese. Then we turned around and began the mostly uphill trek back to the apiary where Don was working with the bees. I led the way as we walked along through the woods. There were no trails. We'd been walking quite a while when it dawned on me that nothing looked familiar. I was worried, but I didn't want to scare my little daughter.

I shot up one of those arrow prayers silently to heaven. "Lord, we need your help."

The answer came, as clear as a bell in my mind: "A little child shall lead them."

I ignored the words at first, thinking they were nothing but ramblings of my anxious brain.

"A child shall lead them."

"A child shall... Hmm."

Then it came again, in the same quiet, compelling whisper, "A child shall lead them."

Three times could not be a coincidence. I knew this was God's answer to my prayer. Nevertheless, I looked at my daughter with a touch of misgiving. "Oh, well," I thought, "I suppose we can't get any more lost than we already are."

Taking a deep breath, I asked my little daughter, "How would you like to play a game of follow-the-leader? You can be the leader, and I will follow you now. Which way do you think the beeyard is, where Daddy is?"

Without a pause, she replied, "Oh, I know. I think it's this way." She took off into the woods, leaving me to scramble behind her.

As she made her way through some heavy brush, I began to see some familiar landmarks. There was the fallen tree leaning just so, the beaver dam, and the huckleberry bush we had nearly stripped of juicy red berries. I felt a huge grin of relief sweep across my face. Silently, I thanked God for his wondrous help and praised him for being able to show his power through any person, young or old. I knew I would never ever forget this day when I needed to remind myself of God's might, his mysterious ways, and the power of prayer. Because of him, Deena was leading us right back up the mountain to Don, the beehives, and safety.

I got out my whistle and gave a loud blow. Sure enough, Don's whistle came through the air in reply. We were soon together enjoying our lunch, especially that icy cold watermelon.

CHAPTER 6

Through the Seventies

*T*hings were going well as we entered the new calendar year of my thirty-ninth birthday. Don continued to build more equipment in our basement workshop, anticipating the expansion of our hive count to over one hundred the following summer. We ordered new queens to put in the splits of strong hives. Splitting worked well for us in those early years. The bees were so strong and healthy then that splitting discouraged them from swarming.

We kept our customers who came to the door happily supplied with honey as well as our few wholesale accounts. But that winter, we did not have enough honey to sell at Pike Place Market. The house sales and wholesale markets were just right for our supply. The honeybees in their nearby apiaries had to be checked every few days, making sure they were okay over the winter.

Had the wind blown a cover off? Had there been any signs of bears in the area? Were the electric fences still working? Was there still enough honey in each hive to last them until spring? We tried to leave about fifty pounds for them to overwinter on. A quick lift of the hive—from the rear, not the entrance side of each hive—clued us in on how much of their precious food supply was left.

Deena Marie was doing well in her fourth grade class at Amazing Grace Lutheran School. Her teacher, Mrs. Hannewinkle, did an outstanding job of teaching—especially penmanship. What a wonderful skill to master! And at the same time, the children were tucking away God's promises in their hearts and minds. I found a sample of penmanship practice tucked away in a letter dated April 8, 1975. Forty-five years ago. The letter which I wrote to my aunt Lena and uncle Luis is a wonderful reminder of God's faithfulness and watchful care. This is what I wrote—nothing changed, verbatim:

April 7, 1975

Dear Aunt Lena and Uncle Luis,

Your voice sounded so good on the phone. You did a lot to cheer me up that night. I'm feeling so much better now—stronger day by day. I just found this paper from Deena's handwriting class at school. That verse was really true when I got so sick and had to go to the hospital. The Lord was with me, and I did not fret because of his peace within my spirit. The Lord gave me the best doctors; I'd never seen either one before. And just to show his love and all sufficiency, the Lord saw to it that all my hospital bill was paid.

Praise the Lord. Tell of his wondrous works. Make mention that his name is exalted, for he hath done excellent things. This is known in all the earth. Cry out and shout O thou inhabitant of Zion. For great is the Holy One of Israel in the midst of thee. I am just overwhelmed. The Lord sent so many to help—bringing flowers, food, and cards—and your long-distance phone call. Also another long-distance phone call from a dear friend in Colorado. The Lord gave her a dream: I was in the hospital. She called Don the night of the twenty-seventh when I was in the hospital.

Mom and Dad came up to see me in the hospital on Friday. I was so happy to see them. They brought along two of my cousins—Bertha May and Esther—who are granddaughters of Levi T. Pennington. They flew out from the East to attend his funeral. I had never seen them before. Did you know that Levi T. Pennington was ninety-nine years old? Deena went back to Oregon with Mom and Dad since it was her spring vacation. It was real quiet around the house last week—which was good for me to rest.

Don was the best nurse and cook I could ever ask for. He did everything he could even though he was still weak from the flu himself. One day, a neighbor came over and vacuumed the house and did some grocery shopping for us. Another neighbor came and fixed my hair. Do you see why I'm so thankful for the Lord's goodness? Today is sunny but cold—not quite fifty degrees. Our garden is coming up; peas, spinach, onions, radishes, turnips, and garlic are all coming up good.

That's all now.

Love,
Doris, Don, and Deena

Another significant thing that happened in 1975 was how the Lord brought just the right people across our pathways. Let me tell you about John Rohrback. He and his family were some of our customers at Pike Place Market. They owned a thriving furniture store called the Furniture Barn. One day, they said they'd like to come over to our house and talk about an idea. We welcomed them with warm cookies and tea with honey. They proposed importing bee pollen from Spain. In Europe, they told us the beekeepers were harvesting pollen for human consumption. It's just catching on over there but practically unheard of in the States.

"I've been importing furniture from Spain with good success," said John, "and I could help you import a barrel of bee pollen right along with my next furniture order. You could expand your sales to everything from the honeybees, not just their honey. What do you think?"

"This is very interesting. Give us a few days. We'll pray and talk it over and let you know," we replied.

So that's what we did. We got a fifty-pound barrel of golden pollen from Spain. We purchased small plastic bags and sealed them off with a heavy paper label stapled to the top: one-ounce- and two-ounce-sized bee pollen—packed by Mech Apiaries. People were fascinated. But wouldn't it be much better to have pollen from our own area and to produce it with our own honeybees? It had never been done before. This was new territory. Where do we start? Have faith. The Lord will provide.

One Saturday, a woman stopped for a friendly chat at our stand at Pike Place Market. She had a nephew named George Anderson who was a beekeeper in Lima, Peru, in South America. He had begun collecting pollen from the flowers by making his bees crawl across a certain gauge screen wire as they entered the hive. And he had designed a pollen trap. We began corresponding with that man, and he gave Don details and helpful advice on where to buy the specific supplies needed to build pollen traps. Now we could reassure our customers that, next year, we would offer them bee pollen from flowers right here in the Puget Sound—not from the other side of the world. This was very exciting. We had to get the news out.

I had some bright-blue-and-gold poster boards made, and I took them around to some of the health food stores in the area. We began wholesaling bee pollen from Spain in 1976 to the following stores:

1. Ames Nutrition—Renton
2. Minkler's Green Earth—Renton
3. Groffs Nutrition—South Center
4. Rainier Natural Foods—Auburn
5. Easthill Nutrition—Kent
6. Groffs Nutrition—Tacoma
7. Burien Special Foods
8. Federal Way Health Foods (later Marlene's Market and Deli)
9. Health Hut—Puyallup
10. Issaquah Natural Foods
11. Nature's Pantry—Bellevue
12. Cook's Nutrition—Bellevue
13. Country Kitchen Natural Foods
14. Cook's Nutrition—Downtown Seattle
15. Brewster's Natural Foods—Seattle
16. Health-Glo Foods—Capitol Hill, Seattle
17. Ballard Natural Foods—Seattle
18. Northgate Health Foods—Seattle
19. The Paper Tree—Seattle
20. 20. The Nutrition Shoppe—Puyallup
21. Sprout Shop—Tacoma
22. Husk-ee Health Foods—Tacoma
23. Health au-Natural—Tacoma
24. Saunders Health Service—Tacoma
25. Marges Health Foods—Aurora Village
26. Pilgrim Natural Foods—Seattle

On days that I was not substitute teaching, I made contact with all these stores to make sure that they were continually supplied with bee pollen. I also discovered a little book, *Bee Pollen: Miracle Food* by Felix Murrat, which I was able to purchase and wholesale to the health food stores.

Don spent his days building pollen traps and checking the bee-yards. He also built a solar wax melter to salvage all the beeswax scrapings into nice blocks of clean golden beeswax.

One day, we were invited to come to the King Television Studio to film a show on bees and honey. We were so blessed with this free advertisement. It was a lot of fun to see the inner workings of a television studio and their excitement in interviewing us with the bees. I was amazed that it took us all Sunday morning to film our twelve-minute segment. I was sad that I had to miss the Sunday morning worship at our church. Our custom had always been to be in regular attendance with all those "dear hearts and gentle people."

That evening, a friend called and invited me to join her in a special service at St. Mark's Cathedral in Seattle. The lead speaker was the charismatic Bob Mumford. I shall never forget it as long as I live. His topic was "The Earth shall be filled with the glory of God." The pipe organ in that majestic cathedral echoes still in my memory. Later that week, I made a banner that hung in our living room: "The earth shall be filled with the glory of God."

Every two or three days, I busily harvested the pollen from the beehives. The pollen traps that Don built were very effective. We bought a large dehydrator to dry the bee pollen. We hand cleaned any debris from the pollen with tweezers. What a tedious job that was! All the different colors of pollen were very interesting. We learned which pollens were the tastiest—definitely the July and August pollens in our area. When the wild blackberry bushes were in bloom, the bees brought in a very sweet, delicious, gray-colored pollen. The blackberry pollen was our favorite. Some customers enjoyed the blackberry pollen fresh from the hive rather than dehydrated. We dehydrated 99 percent of our pollen crop because it kept much longer in that state and did not need refrigeration.

We learned very quickly that one more step was imperative in pollen production. Pollen had to be frozen for at least forty-eight hours to kill any little eggs that a moth or other insect had laid. If the pollen was not frozen, it would come alive, with crawly little worms—definitely not appetizing in the least. As the word spread about the wonderful benefits of the pollen, we were thrilled to be part of this phenomenal growth. People were finding out for themselves how stimulating it was.

Athletes, in particular, caught on, seeing increased stamina. It was great for the circulation. If it's good for people, why not for horses? Sure enough, it was reported that racehorses were amazingly benefited. And the good thing was it was pure food, so it never tested out as a drug in blood samples. We were always careful not to make any outlandish claims, but we were thrilled to share stories we heard or saw in the newspaper. Like the fellow who was lost for several days in the wilderness yet survived by eating wild berries and bee pollen which he had taken in his backpack.

Personally, I found that it was useful in keeping me alert when driving. I drove many, many miles while delivering all those little packets of pollen to the stores. I always carried a jar of bee pollen beside me on the passenger seat in case I felt drowsy while driving. To me, bee pollen was a miracle food. The pollen contained a complete array of nutrients, and I faithfully took it over the years, all the way through menopause, with pleasing results. The work we did to bring it to the public was unbelievable. I wonder now how we ever managed to do it. We carefully packaged it in all those little one- and two-ounces bags and five-and-a-half-ounces jars.

I do remember one little time-saving trick. I went to a local pharmacy and had them help me measure out one and two ounces and then find little prescription bottles that actually held that amount on their precise scale. This step made filling our orders *so* much easier. It was very tedious work.

In the seventies, our pollen accounts to stores continued to expand. In 1976, we had introduced Spanish bee pollen to twenty-six stores. Throughout the seventies, we continued to expand our market with our own pollen harvested by our honeybees in the greater Puget Sound area.

The following stores were added to my delivery routes, with honey by special request:

1977
Crossroads Nutrition—Bellevue
University Village Natural Foods—Seattle
Queen Anne Vitality Foods—Seattle
B and H Natural Foods—Tacoma
Capitol Hill Co-op—Seattle
Fred Meyer—Bellevue
Fred Meyer—Nineteenth and Stevens
Clark's Prescriptions—Bellevue
Auburn Health Foods—Auburn
West Seattle Nutrition—Seattle
Lynnwood Natural Foods—Lynnwood
Nature's Nook—Tacoma
The Food BAG—Tacoma
The Grainery—Burien
Dr. Irene Navratil—Bellevue
Puget Consumers Co-op—Seattle
Greenwood Health Foods—Seattle
Sunshine Nutrition—Renton
Nature's Food Garden—University Way
Alpine Health Haus—Mercer Island
Vitality Health Foods—Kirkland
Howard's Health House—Kirkland
Puyallup Health Service—Puyallup
Ho Bee World—South Center
Natureway—Factoria Mall
The Crumpet Shop—Seattle
The Barn Swallow—Seattle
Carlson Brothers Stand—Renton
JK Herbal—Seattle
Country Village Health Foods—Kelso
J-Vee Round Tree Nutrition—Chehalis
Lotties Health Food—Centralia

1978
Spring Garden Natural Foods—Seattle
Earth's Bounty—Bellevue
Puyallup Health Foods—Puyallup
Natures Pantry—Wieser, Idaho
Image—Issaquah
Keg and Mill—Duluth, Minnesota
Vitamin Patch—Broadway, Seattle
C and B Honey Farms—Bothell, Washington
Rainier Institute
The Health Hut—Puyallup
Way of Life, Incorporated
Practical Pantry—Maple Valley
Natureway Crossroads Nutrition
The Health Corner—Auburn
Wenatchee Fruit Market—Renton
Cook's Way of Life—Bellevue
Honeydew Produce—Renton
Kirkland Nutrition—Kirkland
Alixandr's Nutrients
Boeing Food Co-op

1979
Mari-Don Healthway Natural Foods—Seattle
Culture Blend Boutique
Natureway North
Puget Consumers Co-op—Kirkland
Busy Bee Fruit Basket—Orland, California
Bonn Hatchery—Puyallup
Fairwood Nutrition—Renton
Fred Meyer—Lakewood
Fred Meyer—Tacoma Pacific Avenue South
Fred Meyer—First South, Seattle
Fred Meyer—Lynnwood
Fred Meyer—Greenwood
Fred Meyer—South Nineteenth, Tacoma

Fred Meyer—Broadway, Seattle
The Food Co-op—Port Townsend
The Bon Marche—South Center

A total of 288 honey gift boxes were sold.

Through the seventies when we lived in Renton, we managed 100 to 150 beehives. Don trucked them to different locations in the greater Puget Sound area in search of the finest nectar sources for the bees. The result was some of the most excellent honey found anywhere in the world and such an amazing wide array of varieties.

We produced maple blossom honey; that honey was rare and robust and preferred mainly by the gentlemen. Later, the Corti Brothers Winery in California discovered that maple honey makes a marvelous pairing with Gorgonzola cheese and grapes.

We produced maple blossom honey in the springtime, when western big-leaf maple trees bloomed in Maple Valley. Huckleberry honey—rich, butterscotch, and so aromatic—was produced in June when we took the beehives to Harstine Island and surrounding locations near the water of the great Puget Sound.

July was when it was time to hurry up and get the bees trucked back to the verdant lowlands of the Green River Valley, for here all the evergreen and Himalayan wild blackberries were in bloom. We prayed for sunny days between the July showers, and amazingly, the bees again filled up their supers with delicate, slightly fruity honey from the blackberry blooms.

August was an extra busy month for trucking the bees. Some of them went to Eastern Washington, away over the Cascade Mountains to the high flat irrigated farmland near Cle Elum and Ellensburg. Here they found alfalfa fields and snowberry bushes growing along the fence lines and star thistle. Some years, there were fields of crimson strawberry clover in bloom. We had many wonderful farm folks in that area who welcomed us and our beehives on their private land.

The main crop in August was Mount Rainier fireweed honey. We'd first of all scout out the land and how the fireweed was growing in the logged-off areas. If it looked good and healthy and not too dried out, we'd truck three quarters of our bees up to the mountains on logging roads. Snug in their hive box homes, we'd leave them on the logged-off slopes that were ablaze in color with fireweed flowers. Of course, we'd build electric fences around them to discourage any hungry bears. Then we would hope and pray for the famous fireweed honey flow—the one that old beekeepers had told us about—that happened once every five years or so. When the honey flowed, it really flowed—the nectar literally dropping from the flowers.

And then it happened. The year was 1977. I'm sure the honeybees must have thought they were in heaven. We, at Mech Apiaries, immediately swung into high gear. We drove back and forth with our truck loaded with empty honey supers. That year, we had two apiaries in the Olympic Mountains as well as two different apiaries near Mount Rainier. The bees were quickly filling up the empty supers and waxing the fresh honeycomb off with beautiful white wax to seal in its flavor. We began running out of honey supers. Phone calls to Hobee World and Silver Bow, local suppliers of beekeeping equipment, were futile in buying more supers. They were even sold out of knockdown boxes you could build yourself.

All the beekeepers were scrambling to keep up with the honey flow that year. We finally located a beekeeper in Wells Medina who was willing to let us use some of his brand-new honey supers, shallows, that only had sheets of foundation installed. We agreed to return his new supers after we had extracted our fireweed honey. It was a good thing for both of us. We could harvest more honey and also prevent swarming, and they would have drawn out honeycombs ready for the bees to pack away their next harvests. So we got the bees all stacked up with lots of extra honey supers both in the Olympic Mountains and in the Cascades, near Mount Rainier.

In a few days, we discovered the supers were full. That meant that we had to get to work round the clock. Don extracted the honey in Morgan's little honey house most of the night. Then after a few winks of sleep and a good hearty breakfast, he drove back up into the mountains with the empty frames so the bees could fill them up again. But the honeybees were working even harder than us.

We needed more help on our end of the line. I thought of two friends who might like an adventure: Tim Schlitzer, a policeman in

Renton, and Duanne Smalley, a teacher who was on summer break. Both guys had pickups as I remember.

One day, Tim drove me up to one of our apiaries near Mount Rainier with more empty supers, and we put them on the beehives without getting stung. It's a miracle that I found my way to the apiary through the maze of logging roads. On that very same day, Don headed out toward our bees that were making honey in the Olympic Mountains, returning home with more to extract. More trucking, more sweet success. I still have a little note that reminds me of those days. Don made it and taped it to our fridge: "Whatsoever thy hand findeth to do, do it with all thy might...—Ecclesiastes 9:10"

A couple of days later, Duanne Smalley also drove his truck loaded with empty honey supers up to the mountains, and we found the other beeyard. I'm sure that's an experience he'll always remember. And we had *so* much honey that year. It was unbelievable. It was really unbelievable that Don put his hands to the task of extracting it all. Remember, it was a hand-cranked extractor. And he actually extracted nineteen thousand pounds of honey in 1977. That's the spin that I have so often pondered. Every time he cranked the handle, the combs spun around three times.

But after that marathon workout, guess what? He decided to invest in a little motor for the extractor. It was about time. Don was never afraid of hard work. In fact, it was very satisfying to him to see a task completed to perfection—labels straightly glued onto jars of honey, each jar filled with a precise measure of golden honey. Or in the apiaries, his perfection could even be spotted from the air. Our friend Walt noted this after he flew his small plane across the Cascades. Don's hives were lined up like soldiers ready for a parade.

When Don the Beeman was not working, he chose to be pushing himself to the max in exercise to keep in top physical condition. Sometimes he went jogging around the neighborhood early in the morning. Whenever possible, he got on his ten-speed bicycle and logged up many miles pedaling on rural roads of Western Washington. Sometimes it was a short five- or ten-mile ride but occasionally what he called a "century ride," a one-hundred-mile roundtrip. He lifted weights as well to keep all his muscles strong. Beekeepers are known to have back problems with all the heavy lifting required. So to prevent any back problems, he purchased a book and accompanying cassette tape called *The Y's Way to a Healthy Back*.

Nearly every evening, he did an exercise routine following the regime on that tape. I occasionally joined him on the floor mats. This was an effective way to keep in shape. Our backs stayed strong, and our young bodies were blessed with reasonable health.

However, one sunny Sunday afternoon, I developed quite a severe pain in my shoulder, and it was sore to the touch. I asked Don to help me get a beesting on the sore spot. We had recently read a book about apitherapy called *Bees Don't Get Arthritis*.

"No, I want to take a Sunday afternoon nap," he said. "Forget it for now."

Well, my shoulder was seriously hurting. I decided to take matters into my own hands. I took an empty jar and went out onto our sundeck where we had one active beehive. I got a couple of bees and brought them into the bathroom and had one of them sting me on my bare shoulder. It wasn't hard. The poor bee didn't like being squeezed, and it gave its life in giving me a treatment for bursitis. But I had no idea what was going to happen next. In about five minutes, my face was red as a beet and began to swell up.

I woke Don up from his nap, and he quickly took me to an emergency medical clinic about three blocks away. I was having an allergic reaction—anaphylactic shock. My throat was almost swollen shut. They gave me a couple of shots of adrenaline and had me lie down without moving for at least an hour. A doctor came and told us that this was serious. I had two choices: one, get out of the bee business and stay away from bees as much as possible and always carry an EpiPen for emergency treatment or, two, go to an allergist and get desensitized to beestings. I really could not choose number 1 because Don was so happy with his new job. I was his helpmate, and our bee business, Mech Apiaries, was off to a good start.

The following week, I went to Dr. Baker, an allergist on California Avenue, to begin my desensitization treatment. It took several months of having shots of bee venom. Finally, when he felt it would be safe for me to be around bees again, he said I could bring a live honeybee in a jar to my next appointment. The nurse had the bee sting me while everyone in the office was watching. I did not have any serious reaction for one hour as they monitored me with great interest.

Then Dr. Baker came to me and said, "You are cured! But you'll need to keep up your immunity. Most people come into my office once a month and get a shot of bee venom, but you are in a unique position—on a bee farm. You can have your husband help you get a sting from an actual honeybee once a month. I'd also recommend that you carry an EpiPen just in case you might have an allergic reaction to a multiple-sting incident. Come see me next year. Good luck in the bee business."

For the next thirty-five years, on the first day of the month, I got my beesting, and I never had another anaphylactic reaction. Don was very good at picking up a bee resting on the entrance board of a hive. Sometimes on a warm sunny day, he'd pick up one from the edge of the birdbath where they'd like to line up and get drinks of water. I think he got a kick out of that job because he would often say, "Where do you want it this time?" I learned from experience that—if I ever had a sore knee, shoulder, hip, or any other joint—a beesting would bring relief. In fact, on that very first fateful reaction when I had a bee sting my bare painful shoulder, there was one pleasant surprise. Even though I had a life-threatening allergic reaction, the next morning my shoulder was perfectly fine. In fact, I remember going outside and washing and waxing our Volkswagen. So Donald was able to continue pursuing his dream job with me by his side. I continued cooking gourmet meals for his ravenous appetite. I loved experimenting cooking with honey. We had an abundance of it. I rarely used a recipe but trusted in the Lord's guidance in putting things together.

Like everything else in life, Jesus was the center. He was and is my good shepherd. The thought came to me that I should begin writing all the recipes down and paying attention to the amount of measurements of ingredients I was using in my cooking. So I did just that on a little portable manual typewriter. I quietly tucked the mounting number of recipes away just in case someday they might be useful to others. I shared many warm treats fresh out of the oven with all the good people who came knocking on our door to buy honey. Friends and family heard about what I was doing, and they began sharing with me some of their favorite recipes.

If those recipes contained sugar, it was not at all difficult for me to alter ingredients and use honey instead. I explain those details in the book I eventually had published, *Joy with Honey*. It gives me great joy and amazement now to remember how the first edition of *Joy with Honey* came to be.

One early fall weekend in 1978, I was able to get away for a Women's Aglow weekend. Women's Aglow was a growing group of ladies across all denominational boundaries, Protestant and Catholic, who had been drawn together by the Holy Spirit. We loved our Savior, Jesus. We loved to sing his praises. We feasted together on the promises of God's Word. This was a time of charismatic renewal. And most wonderful of all, his very presence was among us.

I don't remember the speaker's name, but at the close of our morning session, she suggested that each of us should ask the Lord to guide us to someone we'd never met before to go for a walk together in our free time that afternoon. We prayed together, "Ask and you shall receive. Seek and you shall find. Knock and the door shall be opened unto you."

As I was walking out the dining hall after lunch, a lady approached me and said, "You got a walking partner yet?"

"I've been waiting. It must be you," I said as I gave her a smile. "Let's go!"

We walked through the forest trails with tall evergreen trees and lush green ferns at our feet. We walked through swaying beach grass as seagulls soared overhead till, at last, we came to the shore of the Puget Sound. We praised our Savior for the beauty of his creation. Then we shared a little of our own lives and our dreams for the future.

"My husband and I have started a new career. We are beekeepers. The Lord has been blessing our journey as we try to follow his leading and please him in all we do. I do have a dream. And that is someday to have a book with all the honey recipes I've been developing. But my dream is not an average cookbook. I'd like to bring some joy along with it. I'd like to call it *Joy with Honey.* The 'joy,' of course, is God's own word. I'd like to publish some of my very favorite Bible promises right along with the recipes. In fact, I've been writing them out on index cards."

"Wait a minute!" said my new friend. "I work in the publishing department of Women's Aglow in Lynnwood. We have two cookbooks already that are popular with our girls, but we have been praying to do a third book. Your idea sounds perfect. This is definitely the Lord Almighty's timing. Can you call my boss on Monday?"

The rest is history. My book was published in October 1979. It was a joy and delight to work with Women's Aglow in every aspect—business as well as personal. What a day of anticipation as I dreamed of exactly what the book would look like. I finally held the finished beautiful little book in my hands. They actually hand delivered a box full of books, hot off the press, to me at our honey stand in Seattle's famous Pike Place Market. I was on cloud nine that day as I admired the finished project—especially the beautiful cute drawings they had so nicely interspersed between my recipes. I did manage to actually sell some honey that day, and yes, I sold *Joy with Honey*—autographing each copy with a silent prayer that God would bless each buyer with joy in his Word as they read and prepared my recipes. Besides selling the books at our honey stand at Pike Place, I was also able to purchase them wholesale and hand deliver them to stores that sold our bee pollen and honey. Mech Apiaries was becoming known.

CHAPTER 7

Hurrahs and New Horizons

In the seventies as we diligently expanded our hive count, sales, and products made by the bees, we were often blessed with wonderful free press.

The first story was in the May 1977 edition of the *Pike Place Market Merchants' Association News* when Don was the Farmer of the Month. His picture appeared along the observation hive he had built near a humorous sign I had hanging above our honey stand: "We've got the hives." Seeing our story in print brought us great pleasure in addition to bringing in more customers.

The following year in 1978, our hometown paper, *The Renton Record Chronicle*, came out with our story called "A Sweet Business." They pictured jars of our honey all lined up in a row at Pike Place Market and some action shots of Donald and his beekeeping friend, Bruno Lintz, hand lifting the beehives onto our old Galloping Gertie flatbed. Sue Blumenthal, the journalist, had quite an adventure in covering our story. She traveled up in the Cascade Mountains where the bees had made a good crop of fireweed honey. She actually got near enough to the bees to take pictures as well as seeing how they were loaded up for the trip back to the valley to their winter locations. Good journalists, such as Sue Blumenthal, certainly are a blessing and an encouragement to budding new enterprises—bringing in more interested customers and expanding our markets.

The good stories kept appearing. In 1979, we were delighted to meet another outstanding journalist who came to our home several times. She was the unforgettable Peggy Ziebarth. She let the news out that my book *Joy with Honey* was just around the corner from publication. She cheered us on with her kind and well-chosen words in a January 17, 1979, story from the *Valley Living* section of *The Globe News*. The story featured my photo in color at a picnic table laden with tempting delicious food all made with honey. And in my hands, I held a little honey pot and honey dipper streaming sweet golden honey. In the background, you could actually see there was a little snow on the ground behind the beehives near the pond on Jones Road. It was chilly in the air, but our hearts were warmed with elation to know that people were interested in what we had chosen to do.

In 1979, another newspaper reporter came to us requesting to do our story in the *Everett Herald*. On July 21, we were featured in their *Panorama*. This time, they included a picture of our thirteen-year-old daughter Deena giving samples of honey to customers at Pike Place Market. They had a couple of nice photo shots of Don close-up with the bees and getting suited up for the job. Two seasoned guys came to do this interview: Ned Carriek who wrote the story and John H. Davidson who was the photographer. Their insight into the lives of dedication required by beekeepers was unique and thought-provoking. I'm sure it helped the general public have a new appreciation for the jar of honey on their table.

The articles definitely got more people interested in bees and talking about honey. We could tell that this was true by the increased comments of customers at Pike Place Market. They read the papers. Our mailbox was filled with requests from all over the country. Being at Pike Place Market was such an opportune location for us to be. Tourists from all over the country love to see Seattle's colorful and lively world-famous market. A little jar of precious honey made by bees in the Puget Sound of Washington was—and is—the perfect souvenir, the perfect memento to take back home. Like a ball rolling downhill, filling our mailbox, the requests began coming for more. What a joy it is today to reread all those special "keeper" letters which I stored away in a box or two so long ago. Here are just a few examples:

Dear Mech Apiaries,

While visiting my brother in Seattle, we came to Pike Place Market where we picked up a jar of your wonderful huckleberry honey. We've enjoyed it so much. Where can we buy more? We've never tasted anything so good. Could we order more in the mail?

Hopeful honey lovers in Nebraska

Dear Sirs,

There is a crisis at our house! The jar of Mount Rainier fireweed honey we bought at your lovely stand at the market is almost gone. Everybody loves it, from grandpa George to my four-year-old. We live in Mississippi. We'd like to buy more. Please write. (Quickly! ASAP.)

Love, Mama Sue

Dear Beekeepers,

We love the honey gift box my sister sent us for Christmas, with honey made by your bees. They were all scrumptious, but our favorite was your blackberry honey. Can we order more? Can you ship it to Vermont? We'll gladly pay the postage too. We love your honey. Please write. Thank you.

Mr. and Mrs. JS

For forty years, Mech Apiaries was there giving tastes of the wonderful honey their bees produced in the Puget Sound area. Our table was colorfully arranged with golden honey jars and flowers we raised in season. Flowers for the honeybees as well as flowers for customers—one of a kind, custom-made bouquets. Here at our table too was an aura and the aroma of sweet beeswax. Candles poured in our honey house filled a specially designed honeycomb-shaped shelf. And honey in the comb was there for sale too, cut in little pieces and bigger sweet chunks—nature's candy, the best.

Another most amazing thing that happened in the late seventies was the acquisition of a perfect bee truck. It was a new GMC one-ton flatbed, only slightly used. It had been owned by a beekeeper who, before his untimely death, had equipped it with a sturdy battery-operated boom. It could hoist up the beehives from the ground and also the heavy supers of honey and load them right up onto the flatbed. What a dream for a beekeeper.

When we saw this truck pull up and park in front of our house, our mouths fell open in amazement. God was surely blessing us. It's such a wonder how he makes all things work together for good. How did this ever happen? Let me tell you.

Our friend Bruno Lintz, who worked at Boeing, overheard one of the secretaries there talking starry-eyed about a young fellow she'd been dating. His name was John Acton. John's father happened to be a retired minister who decided to take up beekeeping as a sideline career in his golden years. Unfortunately, he never lived long enough to see how beautiful his dream truck worked. So now John's mother, recently widowed, had this truck to sell. We knew John was coming, but we'd never met him before. I looked out to the window and saw him slowly walking all around the truck, definitely admiring it. We walked out to meet him. John was a mechanic working for the Washington State Ferries. He proudly showed us all the details of that shiny red truck and explained how the boom worked. He told us that if we decided to buy it, we could count on him to help us keep the boom up and running. We invited him in to dinner, and so began the friendship of a generous, masterminded mechanic, a man we appreciated so much for decades to come.

In the meantime, we continued operating our thriving beekeeping business right out of our home in the Renton Highlands. Our basement was totally taken over with five-gallon buckets of honey, cases of glass jars and lids of every size, plastic honey bears, a warming tank, and a big stainless steel bottling tank. When Don extracted honey from the honeycomb, he did all that in Morgan's little outbuilding about five miles away. Then he brought it home and carried each five-gallon bucket down to the basement where he lifted it up to strain, pouring it into the bottling tank through a couple of layers of cheesecloth. After filling up several cases of honey bears and glass jars of the different varieties of honey, Don would carry all those cardboard cases up to our dining room and line them up along the wall. So much for a picture-perfect *House Beautiful* setting.

We continued to host many enjoyable dinner parties in spite of being boxed in with honey. I guess our guests graciously overlooked the scene as they seemed to enjoy all my home-cooked meals which featured honey in every recipe, of course. After doing things the hard way for six years, we thought more and more about how nice it would be to have our setup somewhere in the country. We began looking for property—even going out with agents to look at prospective listings.

Nothing we saw at the time felt right. Then one summer day in 1979 as I was driving down the Maple Valley Highway, I saw a For Sale sign for five acres. It caught my eye. I was traveling fifty miles an hour on my way to make a honey delivery to Rubie Spencer at Practical Pantry in Maple Valley. On my way back home, I stopped and wrote down the telephone number on the For Sale sign. The next day, we stood on the ground with a realtor. It was five acres of undeveloped land with a nice meadow in front along the highway. We walked across the meadow and climbed a gentle knoll.

The three of us stood there taking in the view of the woods beside the Cedar River—woods and green trees as far as the eye could see, with Tiger Mountain in the distance. The only structure in sight was the next-door neighbor's small home to the north. As we stood, taking in the beauty of this property, I remember saying, "Don, we'll build our house right here on this knoll where we are standing. I will draw up the plans. Your honey house will be right over there just to the left. You can walk to work! And look at that beautiful meadow. There's plenty of room for a nice apiary of thirty or forty beehives. And my garden will be right in front over there. I'll grow all kinds of flowers for the honeybees and dahlias galore. I'll grow corn and zucchini, pumpkins, and peas and turnips, your favorite. We'll get blueberries, raspberries, gooseberries, strawberries, and currants. And look at the nice hill behind us. Up there, it's sort of flat. Wouldn't that be a great place for an orchard?"

"I do believe there already are some old fruit trees on the property over here," said the realtor. "They were planted by the settlers long ago. Well, this property just went on the market yesterday. If you are serious, I'd advise putting down some earnest money on it right away."

"Okay, we'll think about it and pray and get right back to you tomorrow."

We bought those five acres, our wonderful farm and wildlife refuge for the next forty years. Right away, we dug a well and brought in electricity. Don drew up rough plans for his honey house, and we hired an architect to draw up the blueprints. At the same time, I drew up our house plans, incorporating a lot of designs that we liked in our Renton home.

That home had been built by Bob Miller. We'd heard so many good things about his reputation for building fine solid homes, but we had never met the man. But amazingly, this was to change. The Lord moves in mysterious ways. We were invited to dinner by a neighbor whose daughters had been my students when I taught home economics at Renton High School. Bob Miller was also a dinner guest. We liked the man and decided to hire him to be our builder. He suggested that he could save us a lot of money if I would be the subcontractor to hire different workers as needed. He said he would tell me when to find them: plumbers, electricians, drywall heating installer, etc. We would choose all the finish work—cabinetry, color, carpets, and trim.

It was a delight to work with Mr. Miller—an honest, intelligent, and bright builder. We began construction in the fall of 1979, doing the bulldozer work for both the house, the honey house, and the driveway. Then we proceeded to do the foundation and cement work. Things were buzzing like a busy beehive on our new property. Two buildings being built at the same time headed up with the two different builders. It was very interesting to say the least. We were so thankful to have Bob Miller right there on our property to give us firsthand advice and guidance along the way.

Both the house and the honey house were completed and ready for occupancy in October 1980. What a happy day that was. Moving day. We were finally on our farm. We didn't have to rent a moving truck. The weather was beautiful, and we tied down all our belongings on the one-ton flatbed bee truck. Our friend John Acton was there helping Don load things up, making many trips and whistling as he worked. It was an all-day job—back and forth loading and unloading as I told them where everything was to go in the house. The honey house, of course, was Don's bailiwick.

CHAPTER 8

The Honey Flows

Don extracting honey.

A to Z

Amazing, with anticipation, abundant, alfalfa fields, achievement.
Bees, beautiful, busy buzzing on blackberry
blossoms, beyond our wildest dreams.
Calling forth: all worker bees. With cooperation,
clover blossoms, Christmas berry nectar.
So diligent, delightful, delicious, desirous.
Excitement, eager, expectant, exotic, epicurious
dream, exceedingly anticipated.
A feast to come from flying bees to flowers of the
field and flowers in the forest, fireweed flowers.
Good it is. By God's grand design, greatly treasured.
High gear, happily harvesting holly blossom nectar, huckleberry
blossoms, the honeybee, the unforgettable hum.
So industriously performed, illustriously achieved, the icing on
the cake, illicitly sipped from flowers beyond the baron's wall.
Joyfully jam-packed combs, Japanese
knotweed, jars of golden honey.
The beekeeper's dream, food for kings, knotweed flowers.
A labor of loveliness.
By the master's design, maple blossoms.
Nectars, nature's bounty.
Orderly, outstanding achievement.
Phenomenally, persistently, precisely, patiently, with perfection.
Quiet, quotaless contribution to the hive.
Remarkable, rigorous, radiant with the rising sun, the rush
of beekeepers adding supers to catch a rapturous flow.
Surprisingly sweet, summer meadow flowers,
scrumptious, snowberry blossoms.
Tenaciously, with tender care, such a treat, treasured!
In unity, unique to blooms in a radius.
Varietal with the seasons and blossoms, vigorously
harvested vintage treasures, victory.
Work, worker bees, wonderful rich reserves, *waldhonig*
Extraction time, excitement.
Enjoy zealously, with zest.

$\mathcal{W}$e no longer needed to use Morgan's little outbuilding for extracting the honey. We had our own honey house, a three-thousand-square-feet building. Right away, Don ordered a bigger extractor, a ten-frame stainless steel Maxant. The bigger extractor was there just in time to harvest the last honey of the season in 1980. First of all, the bees up in the mountains, above the little charming town of Wilkeson, produced 750 pounds of honey. This was a beautiful, delicate, light, pure fireweed honey. Our new extractor in our new honey house was christened with this special task of spinning out that crop.

Next came the honey from Eastern Washington. There was an excellent crop there that year in spite of the ground being blanketed with a layer of ash from the eruption of Mount St. Helens. Some beekeepers were wary about taking the beehives to the areas around Cle Elum and Ellensburg and avoided setting them out where the fields were covered with volcanic ash. But we just had a hunch it would be all right. Sure enough, it was exactly the right thing to do. The ash seemed to form a crust around the ground, sealing in the moisture so the desert plants growing wild in that area grew exceptionally well, producing lots of flowers laden with pollen and nectar.

We were blessed to harvest 4,330 pounds of honey from our hardworking bees This was exceedingly and abundantly above all we could ask or think. There was knapweed, sometimes called star thistle, and snowberry honey, over two tons, in the midst of volcanic ash. We thanked God for this amazing blessing. It took Don seven days working in our new honey house to get it all extracted out of the comb. He would get the extracting room heated up to about ninety degrees. We installed propane space heaters which served the purpose of quick, clean heat. Heating the air temperature was better, we believed, than actually heating the honey in a sump to pump into the bottling tank. It was more labor intensive, but that was the way finest honeys were to be handled—with minimum amounts of heat to retain their unique flavors and nutrition. Raw and unfiltered honey was what our customers appreciated. We did not hold the honey at warm temperatures in a bottling tank for days, and we did not warm it more than necessary after storage. As the honey drained out of the extractor, it passed through a strainer lined with nylon netting into a five-gallon bucket. Then Don lifted the bucket up off the floor and hoisted it shoulder height into the bottling tank to pour through a strainer.

When the tank was filled with a specific variety of honey, it was warmed and bottled into jars to sell. Any excess honey was stored away in five-gallon buckets and stacked four deep in the open bay of our honey house. Most of our honeys would crystallize over time in the five-gallon buckets. We reliquefied it by placing the buckets, three at a time, in a water bath with a thermostatic control, stirring every few hours. After the honey was bottled and cases of different sizes were filled, we moved them with a hand truck into our warm storage room and stacked them orderly on shelves. Don believed in perfection, down to the last detail.

And of course, every label on every jar had to be exactly straight. We stamped the variety of honey on the lid after the jars were filled. But putting on the labels was a separate job in itself. He spent an entire day doing nothing but labeling as needed. At first, he used my shiny stainless steel cookie sheet, taking a paintbrush to cover it with label adhesive and then lining up the labels in neat rows before carefully taking each one off to be placed on the jar, holding a clean rag in one hand for a perfect job. That was Don. Later, sometime in the eighties, we purchased a Potdevin labeling machine. This made the job go much faster, but still, it was an all-day job to put the labels on the jars.

All through the eighties and nineties, we operated our apiaries with between 200 to 250 beehives. We wintered them close to home on the eastern outskirts of Renton, in Maple Valley and along the Green River between Black Diamond and Auburn. We had them close by in order to routinely check how each hive was doing over the winter. Had the wind blown a cover off? Had a hive gone queenless? Were there signs of trouble in front of a hive which might have meant a skunk had been around? Was there a highway of ants posing a problem? Was there a lot of chalk brood on the entrance? Was the electric fence still working to keep out any farm animals or bears from getting in the apiary?

All these things were vitally important to monitor, but most important of all was that a good beekeeper never let a hive starve. We always left at least fifty pounds of honey for each hive's winter stores. But in the early spring, their consumption of honey was quite immense as the queen began laying eggs to fortify the hive with new worker bees in order to harvest the first nectars of the year. Every hive had to be monitored for its winter honey stores. So the first task Don would always do when entering an apiary, after lighting his smoker, was to go around to the back of each hive and gently lift it to see if it was light in weight and running out of its food supply.

On an extended rainy spell, when the bees could not get out and fly, he would mix up sugar syrup with granulated sugar and water and fill big black plastic feeders with his supplementary nourishment. Only once, to my remembrance, did we ever lose a hive to starvation. That was such a sad day. We pledged ourselves to never let it happen again. Our goal was to have strong, healthy hives by the late spring.

Mac West, our legendary mentor, always used to say that the test of a truly good beekeeper was how much maple blossom honey he could produce. Western big-leaf maple trees generally come into bloom in the greater Puget Sound area in the month of May.

Some beekeepers choose to truck their beehives down to California to help pollination, but we chose to go a different route. We attempted to harvest as many varietal types of honey as possible, honeys unique to this beautiful slice of God's creation. The following is a chart of how much maple blossom honey we actually produced in the eighties:

1980	1981	1982	1983	1984
maple	maple	maple	maple	maple
1,250 pounds	0 pound	1,000 pounds	200 pounds	200 pounds

1985	1986	1987	1988	1989
spring flower	maple	maple	maple	spring flower
1,025 pounds	450 pounds	1,850 pounds	1,800 pounds	675 pounds

Maple blossom honey is wonderfully robust with a licorice after-taste. It's very light in color, some years with a slightly greenish hue. It's a honey that stands alone, ready to be appreciated on a scone, a piece of toast, or a toasted crumpet. Our friends at Corti Brothers Winery in Sacramento, California, loved featuring it in their signature dessert—a simple little block of Gorgonzola cheese drizzled with our maple blossom honey with a small cluster of grapes on the side. For several years, it was their featured dessert at their annual VIP dinner. It was never a certainty that our first springtime honey would be the treasured maple blossom honey.

In 1985 and 1989, the bees brought in a lighter and more delicate blend of nectars. We decided to label it as "spring flower." Our guess was that they had been feeding on the nectar of wild cucumber, sometimes called man-in-the-ground. This prolific vine was quite invasive in the mideighties and beyond. It bloomed at the same time as the maple trees, so the honey was a blend of nectar.

1981 was a wet, rainy spring. The bees were not able to get out and fly. And when the sun did peak out, the temperatures were not warm enough to produce a nectar flow in the maple blossom. It was kind of like gambling. Don sometimes said, "I don't need to go to Las Vegas." There is always a gamble with the bees. Sometimes you win, more than not, but sometimes you lose, one out of ten in the eighties.

In the month of June, the second honey flow in our region was consistently more dependable for us over the years. It was from the evergreen huckleberry that grew abundantly along the shoreline and woodlands of the Puget Sound. We trucked the bees across the Tacoma Narrows Bridge and set them out on private land on

Harstine Island, Purdy, Vaugn, Home, and surrounding areas. The honey flowed every year.

1980	1981	1982	1983	1984
huckleberry	huckleberry	huckleberry	huckleberry	huckleberry
3,690 pounds	2,940 pounds	5,600 pounds	5,750 pounds	4,250 pounds

1985	1986	1987	1988	1989
huckleberry	huckleberry	huckleberry	huckleberry	huckleberry
3,525 pounds	3,425 pounds	4,150 pounds	4,800 pounds	3,315 pounds

vetch (huckleberry blend) 1,900 pounds		vetch (huckleberry blend) 850 pounds		

Huckleberry honey was my personal favorite honey. I loved its aroma when Don brought in supers of it into our honey house to extract. The heavenly sweet aroma lingers yet in my memory. It was a unique honey as it did not crystallize in storage. I was told that its proportions of levulose and dextrose were slightly different than other honeys, which also made it easier for some people to digest. I'd like to see a scientific study done about that someday. But the real fact was that huckleberry honey was delicious—sort of like butterscotch candy. We had lots of it.

I had an idea, and it proved to be a very good one: "Let's turn some of that wonderful huckleberry honey into taffy." So off I went to Roger's Candy Company on the south side of Seattle. We did just that. People loved it, the young and the old. We increased our product line, in turn increasing our sales.

When July rolled around, we usually had all the huckleberry honey removed from the beehives. The question was "Now where will the next honey flow be?" Mac West taught us to always be in touch with other beekeepers. July seemed to be less predictable. Yet some years, the wild blackberries produced a nice honey.

There are three varieties of blackberries which grow here and which extend the season: trailing little sweet candy variety, the Himalayan, and the evergreen blackberry. The honey from blackberry blossoms is fruity in flavor. We produced a lot of it in the eighties. Some of our customers liked it so much they would buy it by the gallon.

1980	1981	1982	1983	1984
blackberry	blackberry	blackberry	blackberry	blackberry
640 pounds	760 pounds	0 pound	480 pounds	1,700 pounds

1985	1986	1987	1988	1989
blackberry	blackberry	blackberry	blackberry	blackberry
1,900 pounds	325 pounds	875 pounds	2,200 pounds	1,100 pounds

We kept in touch with beekeepers from Olympia to Snohomish County and Eastern Washington. Where was the honey flowing in certain areas? Some years, we put our bets on the raspberry fields near Puyallup. Other years, we would take them farther to the west in Mason County into the logged-off areas of the Olympic Mountains where we got permits to set the hives out on a land owned by the Mackey Timber Company. Here we got a nice light honey that we called mountain raspberry. The hills were covered with black raspberry bushes as well as ceanothus growing around stumps of giant cedars where thick forests once stood.

Later in the summer, we would move the hives a few miles up in the mountains to higher elevations where the fireweed flowers bloomed. We didn't want to miss out on a honey flow to the west or east or back at home. So when we heard things looked good and other beekeepers were having success in Eastern Washington, we would head our one-ton truck to the east and set out the hives there. Maybe they would bring in that delectable snowberry honey, clover blossom, or alfalfa. These were all light, mild honeys. When the bees brought in a dark honey blended from different sources, we called it "wildflower."

This is a summary of the Eastern Washington honeys we produced in the eighties:

1980	1981	1982	1983	1984
snowberry	snowberry	snowberry and alfalfa	snowberry and clover blossom	wildflower and clover blossom
4,330 pounds	2,895 pounds	4,110 pounds	4,950 pounds	5,850 pounds

1985	1986	1987	1988	1989
snowberry and clover blossom	snowberry, wildflower, and alfalfa	snowberry and alfalfa	snowberry, wildflower, and alfalfa	snowberry and alfalfa
3,850 pounds	3,100 pounds	3,800 pounds	3,540 pounds	1,080 pounds

In the month of August, we took several truckloads of bees, snug in their hive box homes to the Cascade Mountains near the foothills of Mount Rainier and also to logged-off areas in the Olympic Mountains to the west. Here on the logged-off slopes, the hills were literally ablaze with color from fireweed flowers. In the eighties, we put them on land owned by the State of Washington. These all required permits and liability insurance in case we might somehow start a fire. Thankfully, we never did. Don was always very careful with his smoker.

Those were the good old days. People never once vandalized the honeybees back then. Nor was it necessary for the landowners to protect their property with locked gates. We did have to guard against another kind of vandalism to our bees though—bear. We always put up electric fences around every apiary. Most of the time, that worked after we learned from experience to place the electric fence far enough away from the beehives.

Those hungry bears loved fireweed honey, and so did our customers. It was praised by Graham Kerr, the well-known host of *The Galloping Gourmet*, and it was just plain delicious, light and mild with a slightly spicy aftertaste. Besides, it was Don Mech's favorite honey, drizzled over his grapefruit for breakfast, just the way Mac West liked it.

1980	1981	1982	1983	1984
fireweed and madrona tree	fireweed	fireweed	fireweed	fireweed
5,350 pounds	6,360 pounds	3,250 pounds	1,950 pounds	7,600 pounds

1985	1986	1987	1988	1989
fireweed	fireweed	fireweed	fireweed	fireweed
4,875 pounds	2,925 pounds	3,175 pounds	7,180 pounds	3,550 pounds

All through the nineties, we continued full speed ahead with our migratory beekeeping operation. There were ups and downs in honey flows and bottom-line production.

In the summer of 1992, we had an unexpected surprise. One of our apiaries in the Cascade Mountains brought in a very thick, dark honey. There was over a half ton of it. Don was very upset to not be extracting more of his beloved fireweed honey. This honey took over twice as long to spin out of the comb. My cousins, Mary and Allan Simon, were visiting at that time.

"Oh my goodness," they said after tasting our newest honey, "this is just like the honey from the Black Forest in Germany! You should call it "waldhonig." And that was what we did. People loved it. Honey connoisseurs I know still have a jar or two in their private stash today, years later.

Our home "yard" and also the Jacobs', Kochevars', and apiaries at Roger and Verdelle's in Maple Valley all produced a surprisingly light and mild honey in 1994. In the past, we had counted on our typical fruity-tasting blackberry honey in July. This honey was something different as it was lighter in color and more delicate in taste. The bees had found multiple sources to blend together in our summer meadows that July. In addition to blackberry blossoms, there was snowberry in bloom, lush clover, trailing cucumber or man-in-the-ground. And on our five acres, there was a linden tree that was a big attraction to the bees as well. We had a new honey to offer. We had a *lot* of it. From our home yard, we harvested 935 pounds; from Roger and Verdelle's place 1,120 pounds; from Ted and Arlene Jacobs, 1,240 pounds; and from our apiary at Joe and Ann Kochevar, 1,350 pounds.

All in all, we had over two tons of wonderful summer meadow honey that year. The blessings kept coming and coming. It was unbelievable! In August, we took the bees up to the Mount Rainier foothills again for fireweed honey in four different locations. Each produced a bumper crop in the year of 1994:

Gale Creek	Meadow Creek	Champion number 1	Champion number 2
fireweed	fireweed	fireweed	fireweed
2,500 pounds	3,000 pounds	2,680 pounds	2,800 pounds

It was an amazing crop of fireweed honey, a total of 10,980 pounds. That year went down in our history as a banner unprecedented year, distinguished for excellence in honey production.

Although the maple blossoms yielded a sparse fifty pounds in the spring, the huckleberry and madrona trees along the Puget Sound and Harstine Island brought us a wonderful 6,725-pound crop. We only took a truckload of bees to Easten Washington that summer. That was the right decision. There, on the Clark's ranch, they only brought in 300 pounds of snowberry honey. We were so glad we had listened to the leading of God's still, small voice and taken four big truckloads to the fireweed flowers.

The honey our industrious bees brought in 1999 totaled to *24,090 pounds.*

In addition, we produced 1,010 ross round honeycombs and twenty-two five-gallon buckets of bee pollen. Whew! What a blessing it was to have good, healthy honeybees. And yes, you are probably wondering how many colonies did it take for us to harvest this amazing crop. It was two hundred fifty, give or take a few.

My father passed away from a sudden heart attack in the middle of this busy summer. Somehow, I was able to immediately fly to my mother's side, and Don drove back and forth to Oregon all in one day to attend his memorial service.

CHAPTER 9

Swarming

*O*ne of the most intriguing facets of honeybees is the swarming phenomena. Like most Americans, I had never seen a swarm of bees. Don had never seen one either, but we had read all about it in Walter Kelley's book, *How to Keep Bees and Sell Honey.*

Swarming is a perfectly natural way that a strong, healthy honeybee colony splits up to form a new home, thereby increasing the number of bees in a given area. For the surrounding ecosystem, this is good and beneficial, *but* for the keeper of the bees, it is just the opposite. In fact, it is a disaster. After all, as beekeepers, we want to keep our bees—not lose them.

A potential honey crop could be lost when half of the bees leave the hive, with most likely their good-laying queen too. The queen's attendants stop feeding her, her usual diet, so she becomes notably slimmer and able to fly. This would only be the second time in her life that she should leave the hive. The first, of course, was her mating flight or flights.

When a swarm occurs, there is a buzz of excitement in the colony. The queen and her attendants exit, followed by anywhere from twenty to thirty thousand worker bees, in a strong hive. They come tumbling out the front entrance of the beehive, filling the air like a dark cloud. Where they land depends on how far the queen is able to fly. This is unpredictable. Over the years, we've seen swarms circle in the air and then head right into their old home. Evidently, the queen wasn't up to a flight that day. On another day, they might all cluster together high up in a tree beyond reach. We've seen them cluster on fence posts or hang like long sausages on low accessible branches. We've even seen swarms settle on the ground. Wherever the queen lands, the worker bees all gather around her.

A few times, we observed a swarm take off like a streak across the sky, flying out of sight to an unknown destination. This is an unforgettable sight but nearly as sad as a runaway child. We worried about their whereabouts. Once, a swarm settled right in the middle of my garden amidst the full bloom alstroemeria. Strangest of all was the swarm that landed on a dead snag. We really were not superstitious folk, but within a matter of days, we were flying in a jet plane across the country to bury Don's brother.

I won't go into all the details of how we tried to prevent swarming in our own apiaries. There are many books already written on this subject. Whenever possible, we always tried to have extra supers on hand, ready to retrieve any swarms in the wild. Ideally, we'd have two outer frames with honey and eight dark wax brood frames in a deep super with the bottom board securely attached with staples. I learned to make the super more attractive to the bees as their new home by rubbing lemon balm leaves on the inside of the wooden box before I loaded it to go.

Back in the early days, we gave our name to the local fire department, volunteering to catch swarms in the community. When our
telephone would ring, we'd get the address, after asking a few brief
questions, like "How high up are they?" and "Tell me, what do they
look like?" With those two questions, we could rule out trips that
would be a waste of our time. We were happy to get more free bees
but not at all interested in exterminating wasps, hornets, or yellow
jackets. Nor were we up to climbing tall trees or hauling extension
ladders.

I remember our first wild swarm. It was hanging on a low
branch of a big apple tree in a yard of what is now called New Castle.
We were ready for that first swarm call—so excited to experience
firsthand what it was like to give the swarm a new home. Don was at
home in the workshop when the telephone call came.

"Would we be interested in retrieving a swarm? Definitely!"

He quickly gathered everything that we'd need: the hive box
filled with ten frames of sweet-smelling foundation—all brand-new;
and don't forget the hive tool. We brought the new soft bee brush
and the smoker and quickly changed into our new white coveralls,
with Velcro straps around the ankles. Our canvas gloves, bee hats,
and veil were tossed into a box in the back seat right next to Deena
Marie and her six-year-old friend, Jennifer, who had come over to
play that afternoon. We were all so excited to see how this would
work, and we all kept our fingers crossed that the swarm would still
be there when we arrived.

You see, a swarm is just a brief stopover place for the bees until
the scouts locate a suitable place for them to move in. Sure enough,
the cluster of bees was still hanging in the tree. We placed the new
beehive super right under it in the grass. Then Don proceeded to give
the branch, laden with bees, a quick jerk. The bees dropped off, most
of them landing right on top of the open super. We watched—fascinated. Would they all crawl inside the box? Don lit up his smoker
and gave the bees around the edges of the super a little puff of smoke.
Then he gently brushed the remaining little worker bees onto the top
bars of sweet beeswax foundation. Next, he very gently placed the
cover on top. Most of the bees were in that box. Wow! But there was

still quite a crowd of them flying around in the air. We stepped back to watch. What would they do next? Then we saw that, at the front entrance of the hive, was a lineup of little workers all briskly fanning their wings.

"Do you see that?" said Don. "It's happening just like we read. They are sending out their scent to call all the family home. Let's sit down on the grass and watch."

One by one, each bee that had been circling in the air flew down to the entrance board of the hive and scurried right inside. It was amazing to watch a swarm of bees in action, orderly little honeybees that would soon be added to our own apiary. We'd been there over an hour watching. Time stood still. This was more fascinating than any television show. Most of the bees were in our new hive box now, but a few stragglers remained up in the apple tree. Don decided it would be best to come back later toward the evening to move the hive to our closest apiary.

Sure enough, when we returned that evening, every last bee was out of the tree and into the hive. Don put a screen on the entrance and loaded it up in the back of the pickup. It joined the lineup at our nearby apiary—another workforce that would soon, in a few weeks, be trucked up to the fireweed flowers near Mount Rainier.

The second swarm call came when I was home alone. Don was out with Walt and the bees, and Deena Marie was in school.

The lady on the phone was very excited. "I've never seen so many bees in my entire life," she said. "They just came like a dark cloud and landed on top of one another in my little tree in the front yard. What should I do?" she gasped. "The neighbors are all scared. I called the fire department, and they said to call you. We are all worried. Shall I spray them down with my garden hose?"

"Oh, please don't do that," I said. "I think I can help you. I just watched my husband hive a swarm a couple of days ago. Do you think I could reach it without a tall ladder?"

"Oh yes, it's within easy reach," she said. "I live on Queen Street," just off Monroe.

"Really? That's only a few blocks away," I said. "I'll be over right away."

"Wow," I thought. "I wonder what I am getting into." Placing the telephone receiver back on the wall, I took a deep breath, remembering the words I had hidden away in my memory. Words from God's own word in Philippians 4:13: "I can do all things through Christ which strengthens me." In fact, those words were printed beside my photo in the Llami yearbook, when I graduated from GFC, now George Fox University, many years ago.

So I did it. I bravely went, all alone, putting everything I'd need in our red Volkswagen bug and suited up in my new white beekeeper's garb. "Lord, I need your help each step of the way," I prayed as I drove to the other side of our neighborhood to Queen Street. As I neared the address, I noticed lots of people standing around, all looking in the same direction at the large swarm of bees.

"Oh, good, here comes the beekeeper," they said. Obviously surprised to see a girl, they asked me, "Can *you* handle that?"

The questions were coming at me from every side. All the neighbors had come out to watch this drama unfold.

I carried the swarm box out of the Volkswagen and placed it under the swarm that was still hanging in the little tree, right on the ground, just like Don had done a few days ago. I stepped back and took a deep breath—silently praying for God's help.

That's when I clearly sensed his small voice, "Don't shake the bees off the branch right now. Take one frame out of the box and hold it right up close to the swarm."

"Okay, Lord, I'll do it."

Immediately, the bees on the outer edge of the swarm smelled the fresh, sweet beeswax and began crawling all over it. When it was completely covered with bees, I quickly and very gently placed it in the swarm box. I took another frame out and repeated the same process until there were three frames covered with bees in the box. The queen was still in the cluster on the tree. A lot of bees were flying around in the air. *Now* it was time to give that branch a quick shake. When I did that, a huge mound of excited bees dropped right on top of the box, and they all began crawling inside where I'd already placed three frame fulls for a start. I waited a few minutes for them to crawl inside. And then after brushing the ones on the edge inside to safety, I carefully put on the cover.

People all around me were clapping their hands. "Look," I said. "I must have done this right. Thank God," I said. "Can you see all those little bees lined up on the entrance board? They are calling the others still flying around to come home. The queen must be inside!"

The people all watched with amazement, and then they too slowly started going back to their own homes. The excitement was over. The lady that called me thanked me graciously for coming, and she agreed to let me leave the hive on her lawn until Don could come and pick it up in the evening. He would load it up on the back of his pickup. For some reason, I didn't want to bring it home in my Volkswagen bug.

Later, that summer, we took that swarm up to the fireweed flowers near Mount Rainier along with the rest of the bees in our apiary. They produced a nice crop of honey. I gifted the lady on Queen Street with one of the very first jars of that prized delicacy. I always thought that it was such an amazing coincidence that the first swarm I ever hived was on Queen Street. The queen bee came to Queen Street.

CHAPTER 10

The Market

*F*or forty years, we were blessed with the wonderful opportunity to be a part of Seattle's colorful, diverse Pike Place Market. We came in 1974, loading up our Volkswagen bug with honey. We were immediately welcomed into a large, embracing, supportive family of farmers, craftspeople, merchants, and musicians. We joyfully learned to appreciate all the wonderful people there—people from all walks of life, people from varying backgrounds, people from other countries, the rich and the poor.

The market is the hub of the city of Seattle. It's where all the action is, especially on a busy Saturday. Just imagine taking a walk amidst thronging crowds of people through this lively, colorful market. Every sense in your body will be brought to life. You'll hear music, everything from a barbershop quartet to country music with spoons and musical saws or beautiful melodies from a piano on wheels.

Every street corner has its musician. The music floats through the air. You walk to a performer on the street corner, pause and listen for a minute or two, then clap, and drop a dollar in the hat on the ground.

You walk shoulder to shoulder with the crowd. But then, faintly at first, you hear a new beat, a new song. You walk onto the next corner, and there again is a beautiful sound—music. It might be a young child playing violin, her long braids bouncing against her calico dress as she skillfully plays "Flight of the Bumblebee." You wonder if she just walked out of a house on the prairie. She's not alone. Mom and Pop stand in the shadows. She's so young.

On ahead, in stark contrast, sits a seasoned gray-haired fellow. His eyes twinkle as he strums a guitar and sings a ballad, a charming story set to music. The people are drawn in, forming a tight circle around him and straining to hear every word of the charming tale he sings. Kids love him too. When the song is over, everyone claps and cheers. "More, more," they cry. He takes off his crumpled brown felt hat and places it on the ground. From every direction, the dollar bills come flying into it, overflowing. Slowly, he reaches over and places his empty guitar case behind the hat, smiling. The bills keep flying in. Baby Gramps sings another tune.

If you listen, you will hear them playing above the sound of voices calling out: "Come and buy, cherry, cherry ripe," "Get some fresh basil today," "No toucha my tomato," or "My peppers were picked just after dawn. Come get 'em before they're all gone."

And the smells. The smells are just divine—mostly. Walking past the open door of the very first Starbucks, you are drawn to that comforting aroma of coffee—so inviting. You are drawn inside for a steaming cup to go.

Then walking on, there are marvelous bakeries with incredible sweets—Piroshky Piroshky, Le Panier, the Cinnamon Roller. Ah! What wonderful smells drifting through the air! The best sticky buns in town. You buy one, of course, and eat as you go, walking through the kaleidoscope of homegrown bok choy, sweet peas, piled-up carrots—a mountain of them. And on the next table, there were colorful bouquets of every color in the rainbow—tulips, lilacs, sunflowers, dahlias, and lilies. Stunning, lovely. You breathe in the fragrant air slowly. And pull out your camera to take a picture.

The sweet farmer behind the table smiles. "Would you like a bouquet?" she asks in broken English. "Only ten dollars with tax."

You can't resist. Her baby coos in his car seat carrier under the table. Smiling, you walk on, asking, "Where do they throw the fish?"

"Keep walking," the young vendor says, pointing his muscular arm straight to the south. "You can't miss it. There's always a crowd. It smells a little fishy too."

"Okay, thanks." You walk on, past sparkling displays of hand-crafted glass that cast rainbows through the air, jewelry, pottery, paintings, photography, and lovely creations of wood—a sweet book skillfully adorned with wood-burned design.

It's truly beautiful. You hand the crafts guy thirty dollars for a treasure to enjoy for many years to come. You walk on and on through a sea of humanity moving very slowly now. There are vendors on every side, vying for your attention. Colorful displays of fruit and vegetables you've never seen before. Stenciled garments hanging in display from the ceiling. Souvenir aprons and T-shirts. You can hear the sound of laughter rising above the voices of the crowd. And then a squeal, a shrill cry. A young lady excitedly steps back a couple of paces, the fishmonger holding a big slippery salmon asks her if she'd like this one. She is speechless.

"Oh, I'll take it," a fella on the other side chimes in.

The muscular young fishmonger then tosses the big fish to another worker. "Shall I wrap it up for you in ice?"

"It's a deal."

"Best fish on the planet! Now who's next?"

Now it's time for lunch, and you are famished. If you'd like to sit down and have a view of the waterfront as you eat, there is Lowell's or the Athenian on the main arcade. Or "down under," you'll find Soup and Salad. Three Girls Bakery makes fabulous sandwiches too, and you can sit on barstools at a counter and talk to interesting people who like to hang around the market.

You might even see a pretty Native American Seattle girl whose name is Ferntree. She walks through the market with a parrot on her shoulder. Or another lady with a determined gait who pulls a wagon with her bunny rabbit contentedly going along for the ride. It's definitely more than you can see in one day. Seattleites love their market, and so do the tourists who come back year after year.

It's the gem of the Emerald City. Although once it was threatened by developers, today it still stands—thanks to all who rallied and voted to "save the market."

But wait. Wait a moment please. You've missed something. You really have. How could you walk through Pike Place Market and not take a stop at a beekeeper's stand? In our city, the market is the place where you can meet the farmer, the real producer. Beekeepers are critical farmers in the agricultural scene.

At least ninety major food crops are dependent on honeybees for pollination. Here in Washington State, the apple growers need many beehives to pollinate the orchards. This is a major source of revenue for many beekeepers as well as the almond orchards in California. But that's an entirely different story. At Pike Place Market, you will find local beekeepers who mostly specialize in honey production. From 1974 to 2014, several different beekeepers came on and off the scene on the farm tables.

The most long-standing was our farm, known as Mech Apiaries. We set up our display on an eight-foot table in the North Arcade at the base of Pine Street. Beekeeping neighbors in our Pike Place Market farm family were Snoqualmie Valley Honey. Each of us seemed to have our own unique niche. In the market, I would say that Snoqualmie Valley was best known for their flavored creamed honey. When someone asked for that, we would always point them in their direction. Or frequently, we'd be asked for honey sticks, those little straws filled with flavored honey or unique honeys, such as lupine or apple blossom. Then I would say, "Oh, you are looking for Marlene. She's over that way." We were competitors, yes. But we were also friends. We all worked very hard.

It took a lot of careful planning and just plain hard work to get the honey, bee pollen, beeswax candles, honey taffy, and honeycomb all prepared and inventoried for the market.

In the summer and fall, there were also flowers to pick and arrange into bouquets the day before market day. For the holidays, we prepared gift boxes of honey in pretty hexagon glass jars. These were quite popular. Our customers also liked the gift boxes with a combination of beeswax candles or a round honeycomb in the center. For those who wanted a gift to mail, we purchased Strauser plastic jars that worked very well. I would always get the Escort or later the Astro van all loaded up for the market the night before. We sold every Saturday for sure and sometimes a couple of days during the week as well. In the peak dahlia season when our gardens were brimming with dahlias and flowers of every hue, we would also be at the market a couple of days during the week.

I picked and arranged the colorful bouquets right in the garden. At the market, we interspersed them among the jars of golden honey. Our table was a feast for the eyes. My prayer for the day as we pulled the van out of our long driveway in the cool early morning was "Lord, may this day be blessed with your presence. May all we say and do be for your glory." It was a joyful job. I usually took along a teenage helper. The kids that I had as assistants were truly the cream-of-the-crop, great young people. They had to be at our farm at 6:15 a.m., in the dark predawn. In the cold winter, they had to dress like they were going skiing. They wore long johns, wool sweaters, cozy warm hats, and thick socks.

We were outside in the cold, all day long, yet at least there was a roof over our heads in the North Arcade. It was a twenty-five-mile drive to the market. I would often remind my helper of how it had once been when Pike Place Market first began in 1907. The farmers came with horse-drawn wagons, bringing their freshly harvested crops to the city folks in Seattle. We imagined them leaving their farms in the wee hours of the morning without heated vans, just to sell in that same location nearly one hundred years ago, where we would set up and sell today. We came with thankful hearts.

Upon arriving at our assigned space on the north end of Pike Place, we would back the van right up to our stall and begin unloading. First, out came the flowers. They made the trip well in black plastic containers which fit into a carrying rack on one side of the van. They were also tucked snugly between gallon jars of honey and bee pollen. Next came all the honey—about twelve cases of one-pound jars, three cases of quarts, a case of honey bears, and two large cases of gallons and five-pound plastic pails, and, oh yes, the gallon jar of bee pollen.

Then came all the boxes filled with our precious beeswax candles—at least a dozen. Last of all, we unloaded the heavy sheets of plywood that we used in our display and the huge honeycomb-designed shelf that would house our candles for today's display.

"Okay now, kiddo," I would say when we were all unloaded. "Now I'll go park the van while you put up the banner above our table and spread out the tablecloth. I'll be back ASAP."

Next, we set up the "bare bones" of our display, leveling off spaces, building different levels, and tying down the honeycomb shelf to a historic market pillar.

Now we were ready for the creative orderly task of arranging all the jars of honey, beeswax candles, bee pollen, honeycomb, honey taffy, gift boxes, and my book *Joy with Honey*. The flowers filled in all the blank spaces. "It's beautiful," we agreed. "To the glory of God." The job was done. "Now you get a treat! What shall I bring you? A hot chocolate or a latte? And something to go with it, of course. You tell me. Here's some ideas: a crumpet with ricotta cheese and gooseberry jelly, a fresh raisin bagel—toasted with butter, a piroshky roll—one with cardamon or cream of wheat inside, a sticky bun with lots of sweet glaze, walnuts, and cinnamon, or a giant maple bar. You are in charge now," I said. "You have a money belt around your waist to make change. There's a tax chart on the pillar for the candles and my book. There's not a lot of people here at eight a.m. yet, so it's a good time to practice your salesmanship. But before I go, let's do a practice run. Here, I'm giving you a twenty-dollar bill. Pretend I'd like to buy two of those cute little hexagon jars of honey for one dollar and fifty cents each. Okay, here's what you say, 'That will be three dollars out of twenty.' Then count the change back to them. You know, we don't have a cash register here. Just take your time. Remember to say thank you and smile."

I was back with our breakfast in about fifteen minutes. We took turns sitting on the high bench behind our stand to eat and enjoy our hot drinks while the other sat on a high barstool at our stand, waiting for a customer to stop. We always gave tastes of the different honeys in those days. We kept the little open taster jars behind a barrier and dipped a long wooden taster stick in for a tiny sample. It was fun to see people's reaction to the different honeys.

Our customers at the market were *so* interesting. People from all around the world come to this famous market. And people all over the world love honey. It was a great unique opportunity for the kids who came along with me to practice a foreign language they were studying in school. And that, in turn, was fun for our customers too.

We were busy all day long, only taking a short lunch break with a sandwich brought from home or sometimes a bowl of steaming hot chowder or a new scrumptious fare from one of the famous eateries. The sky's the limit. Our only drawback was that we needed to tend to business and hurry back to the honey stand.

Closing time of the market was six o'clock, so we began our wrap-up of a busy day at five o'clock. Putting away everything very carefully back into the cases they came in and wrapping each beeswax candle in tissue for the ride back home. We inventoried everything as we packed it away. Usually, we went home with pretty empty boxes and pretty full money belts.

You might think that we would be exhausted after such a long day of work. Actually, it was the opposite with me. After a day at the market, I was always so energized and wound up that I couldn't wait to get home and tell Don and Deena everything that happened that day. My feet and legs were ready for a break though, so we usually went out for dinner on Saturdays.

Throughout the years, over sixty wonderful young folks have helped me in selling our honey and bee products. It's been such a joy to know each one of them and give them their first real experience of what work entails. They were polite, on time, trustworthy, creative, cheerful, and good people. They are all unforgettable.

Deena Motherwell
James Motherwell
Brenda Dumont
Lisa Hearing
Maddie Worsham
Diana DeFrisco
Kelsy Bolton
Alyssa Bitz
Alex Duarte
Madison DeGidio
Blake DeGidio
Cindus AlMansour
Kim Davis
Holly Esvelt
Seth Esvelt
Alisha Boner
Sara Bedney
Aaron Pouliot
Kyle Murphy
Tanya Lintz
Jennifer Rose
Bailey Heinz
Sandra Dumont
Debbie Saunders
Josh Curry
Taylor Sponholz
Alicia Powers
Jakob Kessel
Sarah Gossman
Jessica Richards
Michael Baldwin
Kaylee Holcomb
Margie Fishkin
April Fishkin
Suzanne Taylor
Christopher Taylor

Tia Goad
Stephanie Grant
Mishell Duarte
Liz Ingersoll
Rachael Hughes
Ben Hughes
Josh Huff
Beca Huff
Jessica Buchholtz
Niki Buchholtz
Anna Seim
Grace Seim
Katie Brooks
Karen Johnson
Caitlin Collins
Brian Hearing
Erica Salinas
Kristy Britt
Lynette Canda
Renee Werner
Rachel Werner
Karin Bossart
Greg Olstad
Steve Meador

What a joy it was for me to have all these helpers over the years. They were bright with the sunlight of youth. For most of them, it was their first job experience. Later, when they were ready to get a real regular job, I was happy to write letters of recommendation. After all, they had demonstrated a wide array of skills from handling money to selling a product, treating customers graciously, creatively setting up a display, and enthusiastically talking about everything on our table. I am sure I must have missed a few of them. Please forgive me. It was not at all intentional. Now, in my years of retirement, my heart is very much warmed with thoughts of each boy and each girl. You are spread across the globe now. And two of you are in heaven today, Seth Esvelt and Greg Olstad. It will be wonderful to see you again. Shall we gather at the river?

Thinking back now, over the years, I can remember many farmers I came to know and appreciate. Many of them are no longer with us.

Pete and Miki Hanada were hardworking, talented, Japanese-descent farmers. They grew pretty bedding plants in the spring: English daisies and Johnny-jump-up pansies—a whole farm table full. Later, they grew all kinds of vegetables, including bok choy.

Pasqulina Verdi was as Italian as they come. She had lovely fresh vegetables: sweet onions, tomatoes, lettuce, and big bunches of sweet basil. She fascinated her customers with her witty personality and friendly smile. She brought her own watering can to sprinkle her display and would sometimes sprinkle when someone was too obnoxiously close to her bok choy. She was a kick.

There were farmers from the Philippines too, such hardworking people. I remember Francis Primero and her sister, Carlina, and, yes, another sweet lady named Tina. I always bought fresh lettuce from Tina. Francis and Carlina both grew gorgeous, fragrant sweet peas. And later in the summer, they would have lots of statice in blue, pink, purple, and white. These were everlasting flowers, so they also sold them dried in the winter. And I can't forget the mounds of cucumbers for pickle makers; they grew these as well.

Then for as long as I can remember, there were blueberries across the aisle from us in the North Arcade. Canterberry Farm was owned by Doug and Clarissa Cross. They made blueberry vinegar and wonderful blueberry jam.

For many years, my neighbors to the south were Sabrina and Werner Drier. They had a greenhouse and nursery. Their plants were gorgeous and greatly admired; they even sold rare blue poppies. Their background was Swiss Austrian. Sabrina spoke at least three languages. She also arranged lovely bouquets right on the spot from flowers they brought in five-gallon buckets.

On my right was another Swiss lady whose name was Lucy. She too would create gorgeous bouquets all day from her cut flowers. It was truly an art. People would stand in line to buy their bouquets in the eighties.

I watched them with admiration, and that's how I learned to make beautiful bouquets. But I chose to make my bouquets in the garden from the flowers I grew in Maple Valley. I grew rows of perennials and annuals and at least one hundred varieties of dahlias. In November 1985, I was on the cover of *American Bee Journal* with my honey and flowers. Then in 1991, *Sunset Magazine* came to the market and took pictures of me with the dahlias in September. I was pictured in the magazine for "Dahlia Month."

We sold the bouquets for only six dollars and ninety-five cents in 1991. If any were left over, we'd drop them off at a nursing home or sometimes take them to church the following Sunday. On a good Saturday, I would sell at least sixty-five bouquets.

Sometimes in the peak of the dahlia season, I couldn't fit all the bouquets into the back of my van, so my good friend and neighbor volunteered to fill her station wagon with colorful bouquets and follow me into the market bright and early Saturday morning. That was Caryl Fishkin. What a dear! Both of her daughters, Marjie and April, also worked for me as teenagers, helping me in the market. And their dad, Doug, came over and put up a good sturdy tall fence all the way around the garden so the deer wouldn't eat my flowers and raspberries. We have been so blessed to know so many wonderful people.

There were also many adults that we were blessed to call friends who wanted to experience what it was like to stand behind a farm table at Pike Place Market. It really was a memorable day for them, I'm sure. I hesitate to start listing all these wonderful friends and family, but I must mention the ones who come to mind now:

Dick Taylor
Linda Hartley
Karen Johnson
Linda Zirzow
Barbara Hampton
Leah Pearson
Pearl Pearson
Ernest Pearson
Synove Mathre

Marilyn Green
Mary Simon
Linda Olson

In addition, once a year, the market celebrated its anniversary. All the farmers—well, almost all of them—would arrive at least an hour earlier than usual and decorate their tables, some very lavishly. Ours looked like a float in a parade. We won many awards. Our friend, Henry Morgan, came and helped set up those striking displays, even bringing some of his own garden flowers to tuck into the chicken wire rainbow above our stand. It was always my wish and dream to still be part of the market family when its big one-hundredth-year anniversary rolled around in 2007. And the Lord granted me this desire. Brenda Dumont and I set up our table festively with Don's childhood teddy bear at the center of our display, and we were so happy to be part of that unforgettable day.

CHAPTER 11

Through the Years

*T*hrough the years, there were so many blessings that came to us from our Father's hand. I am thinking now of my book *Joy with Honey*. For ten years, it was in print with *Women's Aglow* and sold over thirty thousand copies. We self-published the second edition with ninety more wonderful honey recipes for the nineties. It was bright golden yellow with a spiral binding. In it, I included a poem the Lord had given me early one morning: "A Touch of Honey." I had been pondering the awesome gift of touch—something I deeply yearned for.

Being the wife of a dedicated beekeeper was sometimes sad and lonely. The bees always came first—even on Mother's Day. But I had learned to be content, just like St. Paul said in Philippians 4:11. Looking to Jesus brought me peace. It really did. But God designed us with a need for loving touch and not just a quick sex fix. Sometimes I did feel very surprisingly fragile. Like the day I was shopping in Safeway and accidentally dropped my purse.

A kind gentleman appeared and said, "May I help you?" Then touching the sleeve of my jacket, he graciously stooped to the floor and picked up all the stuff that had scattered from my purse. I burst out in tears in that store but managed to pay for my groceries and cried all the way home. Could it have been an angel?

A Touch of Honey

A touch of honey,
A touch of love,
A touch from
Someone's hand above.
A touch of sweetness
In bread and wine,
A touch of honey
Makes the common sublime.
A touch of honey
In muffin and scone
Make the honey touch
Your own!
Sweetness to pancakes,
Biscuits, and toast,
Sweetness to drinks,

Even halibut roast.
A touch of honey,
Gift of the bee,
Gathered from flowers
For you and me.

—Doris Mech

In my mind's eye, I'm back now in our farmhouse. It's early morning, about seven o'clock. We've just finished our breakfast, hearty and healthy as always—sourdough pancakes with tayberries from the freezer and a drizzle of fireweed honey on top. I pour us a seasoned cup of dark roast coffee. The rain is gently falling outside. From our dining table, we look out at the beautiful scene. A soft layering of fog hangs over the meadow. We watch the birds coming for their breakfast at the feeders outside the window. Chickadees, house finches, pretty goldfinches, and then a big bossy steller's jay. The little birds scatter.

Suddenly through the fog, we spot a fawn. And then another. They gingerly prance between the beehives, pausing to listen to the hum. Mother doe follows closely behind. They pause just long enough to nibble on the French pussy willow and then disappear into the woods. We love our five acres. But now it's time to go to work. The honey needs bottling, and the stores are waiting for deliveries. We are blessed beyond measure.

The sales of my self-published book are doing well. I wholesale them to beekeeping supply stores, some local bookstores, and catalogs across the nation as well as to local health food stores where I delivered our honey and bee pollen. I also spotlighted them with their bright yellow covers at our table at Pike Place Market.

One Saturday in late December 1993, a young man picked up my book and asked me to autograph it for his friend, Barbara, in New York City. There was no big whoop-de-doo, just a friendly transaction. In a couple of weeks, I received a telephone call from Barbara Anderson, the cookbook editor of St. Martin's Press. She had my yellow spiral-bound *Joy with Honey* on her desk. She said she'd just come from a meeting there where they had all liked my book and was wondering if I might consider signing a contract with them to do a bound edition and bring it into the bookstores. I was elated. I couldn't believe it. But I was also a little cautious.

"Please give me a few days to consider your offer. And could you please send me a recent sample of something you've published? I'd like to see what kind of work your company does."

"No problem," she said. "Just give me your address, and we'll have it delivered to your door."

In a couple of days, FedEx pulled up with a large box of several beautiful cookbooks. I was aghast. What's going on? They really wanted to take on my book. Now I was curious. I immediately dropped everything and headed out to the Maple Valley Library to do a little research.

To my amazement, St. Martin's Press was one of the largest publishing houses in America. I did sign a contract with them. It was delightful working with Barbara Anderson every step of the way until my book finally came out in 1994. It was and is a very nicely done book. I was honored to be one of the first authors to have a book signing at the brand-new University of Washington Barnes and Noble Bookstore.

I didn't go knocking on doors for this to happen. It was truly a gift from above, as it says in James 1:17: "Every good gift and every perfect gift is from above, and cometh down from the Father of lights, with whom is no variableness, neither shadow of turning." I was with St. Martin's Press for twelve years. It was truly fun and amazing to see where my book showed up. They know how to advertise and get books out to the public. It showed up in the Rodale Book Club and the Better Homes and Gardens Book Club and, of course, in bookstores all across the USA and Canada. *Joy with Honey* was published and distributed by St. Martin's Press for twelve years. When I first signed a contract with them, I still remember the song I sang in praise to God at my church: "How can I say thanks for the things you have done for me... To God be the glory for the things he hath done."

There were incredible highs and lows in this journey of publication. It's strange that I only now remember a letter tucked away in my files. It had good news—that publishing rights had been sold to a German company. I would be receiving a nice advance on my upcoming royalty statement. Wow! Was this really happening? My mother always wisely said, "Don't count your chickens 'til the eggs hatch." So I didn't hold my breath on this news. It would have been marvelous to see *Freude mit Honig* (*Joy with Honey*). My German teacher at GFC, Ms. Sutton, would have been very proud. But it never happened.

The answer is a mystery to me, and that is okay because "I know that all things work together for good to them that love God, to them who are called according to his purpose" (Romans 8:28).

Another book was published in 1995 by Linda Eckhardt, *Guide to America's Best Foods*. She came walking through the market one day with an autographed new book hot off the Random House presses in her hands. "This is for you," she said. "I think you'll like what I wrote on page 50."

It really was sweet. What an honor it was to see our name, Mech Apiaries, listed with other best foods chosen in the Seattle area. The list was Fran's Chocolates in Seattle, Maury Island Farm on Vashon Island, Mech Apiaries in Maple Valley, and Wax Orchards on Vashon Island. America's best foods!

Yes, through the years, we have been blessed so many times. Our customers have always been appreciative and supportive. Without loyal customers, a business of any kind just can't make it. Of course, I know that we did have an amazingly wonderful product line, thanks to our healthy busy bees.

In the eighties and nineties, we gradually built up a sizable collection of candle molds as well as molds for making beeswax Christmas ornaments. Every fall, after we had extracted all the honey, we made good use of the cappings wax, and every little bit of beeswax was salvaged when working in the apiary.

We purchased a wonderful machine with hot water coils in the bottom and an ultrahot light which did a great job of melting down the rough wax. The debris went to the bottom, and the lovely clean beeswax rose to the top. An adjustable spigot allowed us to drain the wax into a stainless steel container with a pouring spout. Don sat on a stool and manned the machine while I poured the wax into the various molds. It usually took us from ten to fourteen days to melt all our wax down and make the candles and ornaments.

Before we started, we always covered the cement floor with huge sheets of cardboard. This made the cleanup a lot easier and the room cozier. Usually, we made candles in November, and it could be quite cold. I planned ahead and took our meals to the honey house. Once the wax began to flow, we couldn't stop until we shut everything off for the day.

I loved making the beeswax candles. I loved how the whole honey house was filled with that wonderful sweet aroma that only pure beeswax gives. I loved taking the slightly warm candles out of their molds and trimming them to perfection. I loved how soft my hands felt at the end of the day. And I loved lining the finished candles up on the windowsills and admiring our work at the end of the day.

Early the next morning, I would begin the task of placing the wicking in each mold. We were very blessed for several years, around 2002 to 2010, to be able to use a large collection of lovely German candle molds. The molds were graciously loaned to us by our dear beekeeping friends at Normandy Park Honey, Frank and Susan Fitzpatrick. Everyone in the Puget Sound Beekeepers' Association knew about Frank. He was an amazing beekeeper. He went all over Seattle and surrounding suburbs to catch swarms. He had a unique way of catching them in a special vacuum cleaner that he designed and built. And tales to tell—so many tales to tell. We always looked forward every year to the November monthly meeting of the Puget Sound Beekeepers' Association. It was a Thanksgiving potluck topped off with a gift exchange and then the much-awaited *tall tale bee stories*. You can only imagine. Through the years, we had many wholesale outlets for our honey, bee pollen, flowers, and my books *Joy with Honey* and *Color the Farm*.

The earliest wholesale accounts began in 1974, selling honey only. There was a nursery in Renton, whose name was Honey Dew

Nursery. With a name like that, the owners were easily convinced that jars of locally produced honey would be a plus for their business. Other accounts that year were to Carlson Brothers, Covey's Market, Curt Hutchinson, and Farmer's Market. The following is a history of Mech Apiaries wholesale clients:

Earliest wholesale accounts in 1974 for honey only:
Honey Dew Nursery
Curt Hutchinson
Carlson Brothers
Covey's Market
Farmer's Market

When we started selling bee pollen:

1. Ame's Nutrition Center—Renton, October 1976, 1 ounce, $0.50
2. Minkler's Green Earth—Renton, 2 ounces, $1.00
3. Groff's Nutrition—South Center, wholesale
4. Rainier Natural Foods—Auburn, November 1976
5. East Hill Nutrition—Kent
6. Groff's Nutrition—Tacoma
7. Burien Special Foods
8. Federal Way Health Foods (Marlene Beadle)
9. Health Hut—Puyallup
10. Issaquah Natural Foods
11. Nature's Pantry—Bellevue
12. Cook's Nutrition—Bellevue
13. Country Kitchen Natural Foods—West Seattle
14. Cook's Nutrition—Downtown Seattle
15. Brewster's Natural Foods—Seattle, November 11 and December 8, first to reorder
16. Health-Glo Foods—Capital Hill, Seattle
17. Ballard Natural Foods—Seattle
18. Northgate Health Foods—Seattle
19. The Paper Tree—added pollen books, $0.55 each

20. The Nutrition Shoppe—Puyallup, *Bee Pollen: Miracle Food*
21. Sprout Shop—Tacoma
22. Husk-ee Health Foods—Tacoma
23. Health au Natural—Tacoma
24. Saunder's Health Service—Tacoma
25. Marge's Health Foods—Aurora Village
26. Health-Glo Foods—Broadway in Seattle
27. Pilgrim Natural Foods—1977
28. Crossroads Nutrition—Bellevue
29. University Village Natural Foods—Seattle
30. Queen Ann Vitality Foods—January 1977, added 5 1/2 ounces of pollen jars
31. B and H Natural Foods—added cappings, started bulk
32. Capitol Hill Co-op—5 pounds, $28.50 pollen sales
33. Fred Meyer Nutrition Center—Nineteenth and Stevens, February 1977
34. Fred Meyer—Nineteenth and Stevens, April
35. Clark's Prescriptions—Bellevue
36. Auburn Health Foods
37. West Seattle Nutrition
38. Lynnwood Natural Foods
39. Nature's Nook—Tacoma
40. The Food Bag—Tacoma
41. The Grainery—Burien
42. Dr. Irene Narratil
43. Puget Consumers Co-op—Ravenna, Seattle
44. Greenwood Health Foods—Seattle
45. Sunshine Nutrition—Renton
46. Nature's Food Garden—University Way
47. Alpine Health Haus—Mercer Island, first honey sold on September 1, 1977
48. Vitality Health Foods—Kirkland to Federal Way Health Foods
49. Howard's Health House—Kirkland number 1 at $1.10 and number 2 at $2.00
50. Puyallup Health Service

51. HoBee World—South Center
52. Natureway—Factoria Square mall
53. The Crumpet Shop—Seattle
54. The Barn Swallow
55. Carlson Brothers Stand (Orchards)
56. Honey Dew Nursery—Renton
57. JK Herbal—West Seattle
58. Country Village Health Foods (Kelso)—December 27
59. J-Vee Round Tree Nutrition—Chehalis
60. Lottie's Health Food—Centralia
61. 61.   Spring Garden Natural Foods—Seattle, 1978
62. Earth's Bounty—Bellevue
63. Puyallup Natural Foods
64. Nature's Pantry—Weiser, Idaho
65. Image—Issaquah
66. Keg and Mill—Duluth, Minnesota
67. Vitamin Patch—Broadway, Seattle
68. C and B Honey Farms—Bothell, Washington
69. Rainier Institute
70. The Health Hut—Puyallup
71. Way of Life, Incorporated (Cook's Nutrition)
72. Practical Pantry—Maple Valley, June 1978
73. Natureway Crossroads Nutrition
74. The Health Corner—Auburn
75. Wenatchee Fruit Market—Renton
76. Cook's Way of Life—Bellevue
77. Honeydew Produce—Renton
78. Kirkland Nutrition
79. Alixandr's Nutrients—October 1978, sold lots of honey gift boxes at $3.50 each
80. Boeing Food Co-op Jerry Binkley—1979
81. Mari-Don Healthway Natural Foods—on Forty-Fifth
82. Culture Blend Boutique—Seattle
83. Natureway North—Aurora, 130th
84. Puget Consumers Co-op—Kirkland
85. Busy Bee Fruit Basket—Orlando, California

86. Bonn Hatchery—Puyallup
87. Fairwood Nutrition—Renton
88. Fred Meyer—Lakewood, 1977
89. Fred Meyer—Tacoma Pacific Avenue South
90. Fred Meyer—Seattle First South
91. Fred Meyer—Lynnwood
92. Fred Meyer—Greenwood
93. Fred Meyer—Tacoma, South Nineteenth
94. Fred Meyer—Broadway, Seattle
95. The Food Co-op—Port Townsend, 1979
96. The Bon Marche—South Cent

In November, *Joy with Honey* was in print and wholesaled to stores, and in 1979, 288 honey gift boxes were sold at $3.90 each, in total of $1,123.00.

97. DeCor Carpets—1980
98. C and R Natural Foods—Yelm
99. Bob's Quality Meats—West Seattle
100. The Pacific NW Shop
101. Madison Square Gardens—Seattle, October, moved to Maple Valley
102. Dr. Baker—Burien
103. Manna Natural Foods (Cle Elum)—*Joy with Honey*, Second Edition
104. Pike Place Natural Foods—retailed at $3.95
105. Nutrition World—114th Avenue Southeast, Kent
106. Tenzing Momo—Seattle
107. Green Earth—Renton
108. Natureway—Federal Way
109. Health Pantry—Bellevue
110. Health Pantry—Kirkland
111. Peckenpaugh Hallmark—Auburn
112. Enumclaw Nutrition
113. Health Pantry—Moses Lake
114. Lakewood Co-op—Tacoma, 1981

115. Lunds Lites
116. Independent Fisherman's Packing Company (Anacortes)
117. Westgate Health Foods—Tacoma
118. PTL Co-op—Renton
119. Herbal Pantry—Federal Way
120. Central Co-op—Seattle Twelfth and Denny, 1982
121. PCC—Greenlake
122. Parkland Nutrition—Tacoma
123. Fresh and Ripe—Renton Shopping Center
124. Capitol Hill Co-op—Twelfth and Denny
125. Des Moines Health Foods—May 1982, good news on our pollen
126. Health Pantry—Wenatchee, was tested by the University of Washington lab, and it's pesticide-free
127. Kailua Health Foods—Hawaii
128. Seattle First Natural—Sixth
129. Beekeepers Farms—September 1982, sold totes for $6.75 with four 16 ounces Strauser jars of honey and for $7.15 in November.
130. Mother Earth (Queen Anne)—1983
131. Country Kitchen—West Seattle
132. Health Pantry—Burien
133. Clark's Prescriptions—Kent
134. Nutritionally Yours—Renton
135. Garden Grocer—University Way
136. Host International—Seattle-Tacoma International Airport, July 1983, $8.50 for six wooden honey totes, $6.00 for thirty-six gift box honey and August 12, wooden totes and six honey gift boxes
137. Plateau Blueberries—Redmond
138. The Best of All Worlds—Seattle
139. Gourmet's Pantry—Tacoma Avenue Noth
140. Maple Valley Food Center
141. Maple Valley Shell—twenty-two new wholesale in 1984
142. Sur La Table—Seattle
143. Made in Washington—Pike Place Market

144. Country Manor—Edmand's
145. Aldrich's—Port Townsend
146. The Pastry Case—Wallingford
147. Kathleen's—First Avenue Seattle
148. Hobart Store—Hobart
149. AW Pearce—Fruit Stand Maple Valley Highway
150. Harp Cheese and Sausage—Black Diamond
151. Sabrina's Bistro—Redmond
152. Godsway Co-op
153. The Feed Store—Gillman Village, Issaquah
154. Taste the Northwest—Gillman Village, Issaquah
155. Tiger Mount Country Store
156. Ralph's Thriftway—November 1984
157. Bendy's Country Kitchen—Renton Shopping Center
158. The Golden Blend—Kent
159. Black Diamond Bakery—Black Diamond
160. Culinary Connection
161. Blossom Boutique
162. Corti Brothers—Sacramento, California, 1985
163. John Ash and Company—Santa Rosa, California
164. Chinook Waldorf School
165. Vita-King Nutrition—Chehalis
166. Nutri Mart—Chehalis
167. Lottie's Health and Diet—Centralia
168. Auburn Pharmacy
169. Johnny's Grand Central—Covington
170. The Dough Shop—Maple Valley in May
171. Bernie's Produce—Auburn, started selling
172. Sha-Ryns Market—Renton, huckleberry honey taffy
173. Sorenco Hotel—Seattle
174. Y and Y Farms—Fife
175. Eaton's Service—Maple Valley
176. Roadside Candy—Burien
177. Gourmet Unlimited—Mercer Island
178. Tahoma HS Holiday Home Tour
179. Larry's Markets—Seattle, 1986

180. Bee Barn—Puyallup
181. Johnny's East Hill—Kent
182. The Gift Basket
183. Gourmet Unlimited
184. Highland SeaFood—Seattle
185. Nutrition World—Kent
186. Apple Barrel Country Store—Kent
187. Seattle Sheraton Hotel—Seventh at Pike Place Market
188. Yakima Fruit—Snohomish
189. Frank's Meat Market—Black Diamond
190. The Cheese Factory—Tacoma
191. Don's Quality Products—Renton, September 1986
192. Marlene's Market and Deli—changed name
193. Brie and Bordeaux—Seattle
194. For Your Health—Kent
195. Sandi's Gift and Basket—Morton
196. Fireside Flowers and Gifts—Vancouver, Washington
197. Valley Harvest—Fairwood, 1987
198. Larry's Markets—Pacific Highway South
199. Larry's Markets—Roxbury
200. Larry's Markets—Westminster Way North
201. Larry's Markets—Aurora North
202. Greenlake Deli
203. The Candy Basket of Centralia
204. Diana's Herbs—Kent
205. Snohomish Books
206. John Ebsary—Maple Valley
207. Summit Inn—Maple Valley, honey and flowers
208. Sunshine Corner—Kent
209. Admiral Thriftway—Forty-Second Southwest, Seattle
210. Queen Anne Thriftway
211. Johnny's PX Plus
212. Artist Workshop—Tacoma, 1988
213. Group Health Teal Café—Seattle
214. Ballard Market
215. The Good Little Food Store—Issaquah

216. Plaza Nutrition—Puyallup
217. Ebrû—Crossroads
218. Market Ventures—Pike PL Catalog
219. Ebisu Trading Company
220. Task's Unlimited—Kent
221. Canyon Road Feed—Puyallup
222. Munson's Nutrition—Tacoma
223. Green Valley Meats—Auburn
224. Brenner Brothers—Bel-Red Road
225. DeLights—Tacoma
226. Nature's Pantry—Tenth Street Bellevue, 1989
227. Red Apple Market—Maple Valley
228. Country Store—Anacortes
229. Ratz 'n Fratz—Kent—They liked honey fudge sauce.
230. Whole Foods Market—Gig Harbor
231. Country Goose—Anacortes
232. Whole Foods Market—Tacoma
233. Enumclaw Fruit Stand
234. Anacortes Health—Anacortes
235. Living Foods Dehydrators—Fall City
236. Abundant Life Nutrition—Mercer Island, 1990
237. Pilgrims Garden Grocer—University Way
238. Main Street BP—Chehalis
239. Many Visions—Cle Elum
240. Long Acres—Renton, ten bunches of dahlias
241. Happy Valley Farms—Anacortes
242. Carol's Maple Valley Floral—1991
243. Chitek Incorporated—Bothell, Washington
244. Tony's Market—Burien
245. Simpler Times—Maple Valley
246. Nutrition Etc.
247. B-Hive Per Pollen Company—Dardanelle, Arkansas
248. 4 Corners Espresso—Maple Valley
249. Burdic Feed—Kent
250. Zerr's Feed Store—Kent
251. Gloria's Restaurant—dahlias

252. Dinner House—dahlias
253. REI—Seattle—thirty-five 2 ounces hexagon jars of honey
254. Countryside Nursery—Kent
255. Your Health Incorporated—Kent
256. Nature's Pantry—Mercer Island
257. Greenwood Price Chopper—Greenwood featured in *Country*
258. Shoreline Price Chopper—1992, mail orders
259. Basket Coat—Bellevue soared
260. Espresso Pacifico Limited—Wilmette, Illinois, mailed twenty cases of honey to Corti Brothers in Sacramento; not a jar was broken.
261. Tea House Café—Issaquah
262. Sweet Basil and Time—Maple Valley
263. Trivia and More—Gilman Boulevard, Issaquah
264. Walla Walla College—forty-two gift sets sold
265. Rogers Elementary School—Walla Walla, twenty-two gift sets
266. Palmer Coking Coal Company—Black Diamond
267. Nature's Market—Kent, 1993
268. QFC—Maple Valley
269. Gift Baskets by Novelle—Tacoma
270. My Sisters Produce—West Friendship, Maryland
271. Village Drug—Maple Valley
272. Hein's Designs—Mount Vernon, Washington
273. Trees and Bees—Auburn
274. Hap's Books—Maple Valley
275. Musquaw Books—Renton
276. Newton's Christian Books—Renton
277. Ricardo's Juice Bar—Seattle
278. Five Corners Nursery—Seattle
279. Mann Lake Supply—Hackensack, Minnesota
280. The Beez Neez Apiary Supply—Snohomish, Washinton
281. Dadant and Sons, Incorporated—Hamilton, Illinois
282. Molbacks Seattle Garden Center

283. Evangel Book Store—Bellevue
284. Genesis Book Store—Kent
285. Second Story Bookstore—North Forty-Fifth, Seattle
286. Aid Association for Lutherans
287. North Peace Apiaries—Fort St. John, British Columbia
288. Evergreen Baskets—Maple Valley
289. Brushy Mount Bee Farm—North Carolina, 1994
290. St. Martin's Press—New York
291. Health Synergy
292. The Brew by You—Shelton
293. QFC—Covington
294. Enchanted Winds Christmas Trees—Hobart
295. Domani Restaurant—Bellevue
296. The Sport Shop
297. Cascade Ginseng Farms—Seattle, 1995
298. General Nutrition Center—Kent
299. Natural and Natural—Tacoma
300. Keim Family Market—Seaman, Ohio
301. Issaquah Brew House—Eagle River Brewing Company
302. Hen Sen Herb Company—Seattle
303. Marlene's Market and Deli—Tacoma, Thirty-Eighth
304. Willow's Nutrition Shoppe—Puyallup
305. Nature's Own—Issaquah
306. Korean Ginseng Center
307. Mother Nature's—Seattle First Avenue, 1996
308. Maple Valley Bakery—four corners
309. Evergreen Health Pantry—Bellevue
310. University Natural Foods
311. Seabird Video—Maple Valley
312. Your Health—Puyallup
313. Village Books and Beans—Maple Valley
314. GNC—Panther Lake
315. Maple Valley Market and Nutrition Center
316. The Crusty Loaf—Seattle
317. Natureway—West Seattle, 1997
318. Natureway—Downtown Seattle

319. Ever Young Incorporated—Issaquah
320. Franz Bead Company—Shelton
321. Jeffrey Steingarten, *Vogue* magazine—New York
322. Western Ale and Brew Pub—Seattle-Tacoma
323. Natureway—Northgate Mall
324. Eirs Owl Pantry—1998
325. Foss Market—Covington
326. Pike Place Market CSA—1999
327. Farm Fresh Produce—Maple Valley
328. Northwest Café, Group Health—Renton
329. The Herbalist—Seattle, 2001
330. Lande Feed—Maple Valley, 2002
331. Glorybee—Eugene, Oregon
332. Bees in the Burbs—Maple Valley
333. BeeKind—Sebastopol, California
334. Food Concepts—Seattle

Our last wholesale opportunity was amazingly to a company called Food Concepts. They purchased fifty-five pretty little hexagon jars of our Mount Rainier fireweed honey for each of the governors attending the 2004 Governor's Convention in Seattle.

CHAPTER 12

Whatsoever Things Are Lovely

WASHINGTON
HONEY
FROM THE BEES OF:
MECH APIARIES
P.O. Box 452
MAPLE VALLEY, WA
98038

*L*iving in the country was lovely. We so much appreciated driving home after a day in the city to be greeted with green trees and green-colored hillsides. The trees formed an arched canopy across the Maple Valley Highway in the old days. I'll always remember the wild cherry trees near the Cedar River. Their cherry blossoms announced that it was spring. And on our five acres, we walked in the woods seeing how many trilliums were in bloom under the big cedar tree. At the edge of the meadow out front, the Japanese quince bush bloomed in bright hot pink, attracting hummingbirds.

Spots of yellow appeared under the bare silver maple sprinkled with shades of blue—daffodils and woodland hyacinths planted by someone decades ago who lived in this beautiful land. Every season was lovely. Summer with the rose arbor bursting in color and daisies in the meadow, soon to be followed by our one-fourth-acre garden in full bloom. I grew many different flowers that were attractive to the honeybees. Some of their very favorites were anise hyssop, sunflowers, black-eyed Susans, bee balm, alstroemeria, and sedum. The garden was my delight. I loved tending the soil, planting, pruning, watering, and, yes, even weeding. It was always a special day when the family came to help in the garden.

I loved designing pathways and making inviting cozy places for a cup of sweet ice tea on a nice day, with my daughter and grandkids or a friend. For seven years, I hosted a gala garden party. We called it Harps in the Garden. On the first Friday of August when the dahlias were in their glory, I invited my friends to come and see the garden—to sit and sip lemonade or blackberry punch with cookies and to listen to heavenly harp music. Actually, a harp trio of a friend I'd known since the early sixties, Gail McEwen; her sister, Mary Webb; and neighbor friend, Maria Wilson. They called themselves the MGM Trio. I am so grateful to all the dear friends who came to my side to bring this event together. Gaylord and Sharon Schroeder brought pop-up canopies for shade, and John and Dianne Hearing brought more. Our friend, Bill Sloan, helped immensely setting it up and loaning us tables and chairs.

My sister, Marilyn, came all the way from Oregon with her glass party trays and cups and punch bowl to help make sure the garden was ready and we were ready for a party. My grandkids came to blow up balloons and enjoy the afternoon too. Friends came from Bible Study Fellowship, the YMCA, from church, and family from far and near as well. There were sixty people who came in 2018—our Seventh Annual Harps in the Garden. It was the last one to happen at our farm in Maple Valley. Lovely memories I will always cherish. And memories I will always keep and look at again and again in the lovely photo book made by John Hales. He took many beautiful pictures of the flowers and the people in 2015, 2016, and 2017.

Loveliness comes in many forms: in photography capturing lovely scenes, in artwork, in well-planned order and the lack of clutter, in dance and movement, in music, and in yet more—the glow of a happy face touched with God's presence. And the loveliness of family and friends bonding together in friendship, koinonia. Our daughter Deena Marie is a gifted artist. She helped us out so much drawing our label and illustrating the coloring book we had published in 2007, *Color the Farm*.

Sometimes one does not really appreciate the loveliness of order: jars of honey lined up straight in a row, their shades of light gold to darker hue enhanced by warm light from behind. That is loveliness.

Surprisingly, if you stop to notice and think about it, there is loveliness in a woodpile. Not one that has been haphazardly thrown together, but one like Don—the perfectionist, down to the last detail—made. First, every log or branch from a fallen tree had to be measured and cut precisely using a measuring stick. Then only stacked as he could do it, with an eye for perfection. It was a thing of beauty! Yes, a simple woodpile.

I have not told you about all the swarms that got away; all the bears that came for dinner in the apiary; all the hives that got shot up for target practice or, worse yet, rammed to splinters with a macho, big pickup; galloping Gertrude the Bee Truck breaking down in the middle of the night loaded up with bees; and coming to an apiary to find half of the hives taped shut with ducting tape—obviously, the would-be thieves were unaware of the upper entrance, so they hopefully got stung up pretty good before being able to go through with their evil plans. Nor have I mentioned being robbed of our cashbox at the end of a good day at the market or, worst of all, having our six last remaining beehives poisoned when feeding on the flowers of Japanese knotweed along the Cedar River. Some people considered eliminating noxious weeds more important than letting honeybees live.

I have chosen to remember the good things, mostly the good times. Times with the happy hum of honeybees, when the honey flowed, and we lived on five acres in beautiful Maple Valley.

CHAPTER 13

2002: A Year to Remember

But beauty is fleeting. Things change. The sunlight of youth and strength of manhood will one day end. How it ends is God's design.

One cold December afternoon in 2001, we went for a walk on the railroad tracks to look at the raging floodwaters of the Cedar

River near our home. We had only walked a short distance when Don experienced chest pains and dizziness. We walked very slowly back home, and he went straight to his La-Z-Boy and sat down.

I called my neighbor, Gladys.

"Sounds like something serious," she said. "Better get him to the doctor ASAP."

The next day, we were in Group Health, now known as Kaiser Permanente, in Redmond. Tests revealed that he had serious problems with his heart. It was Christmas Eve when we received the news that, a couple of days later, he'd be having an open-heart surgery after the holidays. We were in a state of shock.

Somehow, we managed to get through Christmas, but he sat like a zombie, refusing to open his Christmas gifts that we placed on his lap to be joyfully opened.

His mind must have been on the bees. "What will we do with the bees?" he said. "I know I won't be able to care for two hundred beehives anymore."

"Yes, let's face it," I said. "We should sell some of the hives. You can't handle such a big workload anymore."

We got the word out, advertising "Beehives for sale. Call with your best offer."

Beekeepers came all the way from Montana to Vancouver as well as many local Washington beekeepers to buy strong, healthy hives. We brought our hive count down by about one-half.

We also realized that it would be impossible for us to continue our large delivery routes to all the stores over the Puget Sound. Don no longer would have the stamina to keep up with his end of the line, which was labelling all the jars and filling them with our honey and then stacking them in the warming room ready for me to do the deliveries. Here again we went to our friends. Frank and Susan Fitzpatrick were happy and eager to take over most of our wholesale accounts. We decided to just keep up with a select few as long as possible: Marlene's Market and Deli, Nature's Pantry, Practical Pantry, QFC in Maple Valley, and the Black Diamond Bakery.

Frank was such a hard worker. In addition to his Boeing job, he and Susan did a great job keeping the health food stores supplied with their honey. Besides that, remember he was the guy who was known all over the area for catching swarms. He was just amazing. We were all very shocked and saddened when we received the news a couple of years later that he had died of a massive heart attack in the beeyard with other beekeepers from Puget Sound Beekeepers' Association. They had slept in tents in a picturesque apiary in Enumclaw the night before, planning to load up the beehives very early the next morning to take them to the fireweed flowers near Mount Rainier.

Don was blessed to have his heart condition diagnosed by the fine doctors and medical team at Group Health. He had an open-heart surgery—a double bypass and a new cow's valve. He was given a new lease on life.

It was a slow but determined road to recovery. When he came home from the hospital, he was told to lift no more than ten pounds for the first six weeks. You can only imagine what a challenge that was for a once-tough "I can do it myself" beekeeper.

I don't know now how we ever did it. But I'm sure it was with the Lord's help and many friends and family who pitched in with the lifting. There were so many things to lift. We never thought about it before. Take the big car batteries for example. These had to be lifted and hooked up to a charger in the honey house before being taken to the apiaries, replacing the old ones. So he asked me to do it. Yikes! This was so scary to me. He might as well have asked me to hook up the sun to the moon. I could do lots of things, believe me, but anything slightly mechanical was not in my ballpark. But I did it anyway. Duty called.

Our son-in-law, Max, rode along in the truck with Don to check up on all the apiaries. Max was able to replace the batteries in the electric fences as Don did the coaching. Max did the lifting. That year, he was blessed with so many wonderful friends and family who were able to take time out of their busy lives to come and help a beekeeper in need. John Acton, Bruno Lintz, Dima Banin, Brandon DuMont, Matt Olstadt, Frank Fitzpatrick, and Bill Sloan all came, and also friends from the Puget Sound Beekeepers' Association, to name a few.

It was not a mere coincidence when someone drove up our driveway. The Lord, our good shepherd, clearly arranged it just at the right time. "My help is in the name of the Lord, who made heaven and earth" (Psalm 124:8). You see, we had to periodically do some very heavy lifting when it was time to put more honey in the jars. Those five-gallon buckets of crystallized honey, weighing sixty pounds, had to be lifted on the hand truck into the warming tank and then lifted up again to be poured into the bottling tank.

Don could not do it. It was too heavy for me too. I certainly didn't want to tweak my back. So when the nice deliveryman or plumber or friend appeared at the opportune time, they were all kindly asked and willing to loan us a hand. And they were more than happy to receive a jar of honey in return.

After Don's open-heart surgery, he was so eager to build up his strength again. I cooked him a heart-healthy Mediterranean diet, and he was careful to follow doctors' orders on no lifting, but exercising was important. First, he walked laps in circles inside our house. Then he progressed to doing the stairs down to the basement where he got on his exercise bike for a twenty-minute ride. Later when the weather was nice, he would walk around our honey house on the circular driveway, using a cane at first. By April, the doctors said he could drive again, so he began going for walks on the lovely nearby Soos Creek Trail. One day, he ran across a familiar face. It was Wayne Schneider, the beekeeper and farmer owner of HoBee World in South Center. They became walking buddies. As he felt stronger day by day, he also longed to be up in the mountains again. He settled for Mount Peak in Enumclaw. Before the year 2002 had ended, he climbed on that trail twenty times. Of course, at first, only partway to the top. His goal all along was to get back to his first love—the bees. Miraculously he achieved that goal. By the goodness and grace of God and with the help of many beekeeping friends in 2002, the year of his open-heart surgery, we produced 5,565 pounds of honey with the one hundred or so hives we had left:

maple blossom, 95 pounds
huckleberry, 2,560 pounds
blackberry, 1,130 pounds
snowberry, 185 pounds

mountain flower, 275 pounds
fireweed, 1,320 pounds
5,565 pounds total

In addition to the extracted honey, we also produced 179 rounds of honeycombs and several shallows of cut comb honey.

Somehow, we were able to do all that. But Don was a bear to live with. It was such a blessing for me to be able to get away from the house on Saturdays to set up our table at Pike Place Market. I only came on Saturdays, and more often than not, I came alone, without a teenage helper. Since we had eliminated the bulk of our store accounts, we were watching every penny. I took advantage of the fellows who were looking for an extra buck hanging around the market. I paid them four bucks to unload for me in the morning and four more bucks in the evening to load up at the end of the day.

In my files is a letter written to my mother on June 23, 2002, after one of those Saturdays which I went to the market alone:

Dear Mom,

Yesterday at the market was awesome. I will never forget two specific incidents. One was a young man who was in a wheelchair. He had no hands or feet, and his nose was a plastic job—you could tell. But he was the most incredibly joyful and outgoing individual. His brother was with him. They purchased beeswax candles, a pair of turkeys for their mother, and another pair of short ones. They were from Minnesota.

Then, at the end of the day, I noticed a very handsome traveler just sitting on the corner of the back bench and watching my things when I returned from getting my van to load up. There were also three rough-looking young thugs hanging around. I went ahead and began loading up with the man who always helps me load—never speaking to the traveler but looking into his eyes as I passed by, carrying boxes. He was so handsome. I was feeling a little embarrassed that he was watching, so I walked around the other side of the van with my next load. When I came back to get the next load, he had disappeared from sight, and so had the three thugs. There was no one else in the market except the man helping me load up. I think the handsome traveler must have been an angel.

Love,
Doris and Don

By April, Don had recovered enough from his open-heart surgery to begin beekeeping again. He was sure happy about that. He ordered new queens and made splits, putting the new queens in four-frame nucs. Then when they were built up strong, he introduced those frames into a full-sized hive. And before the month of April was over, he was driving down to the apiaries by the Green River to add supers for the blackberry honey flow. When it was time to pull the honey, there was always someone who went along with him to do the heavy lifting.

Dima Banin, Bruno Lintz, Bill Sloan, Brandon DuMont, and Matt Olstad each went along with him, true friends indeed. They were a godsend because he surely could not have done the heavy lifting required. Our good friend, Ernie Fuhr, from North Peace Apiaries in the Peace River Valley of British Columbia, also came to visit us periodically. Sometimes he brought us some of his fine bee pollen, which we blended with ours.

Dave Noonan, from Massachusetts, was another beekeeper, who Don thoroughly enjoyed visiting with and hanging out together in the beeyard whenever he was in town. His daughter, Ann, owned the Pantry Case in Wallingford. Beekeepers were always welcome in our home, just like the closest of kin.

Once, it was our great delight to host Charlie Mraz, who helped establish the American Apitherapy Society. I'll never forget when we were having dinner at Ivar's on the Seattle Waterfront that he pulled out a little jar of honey from his pocket. This gentleman could not enjoy a meal anywhere without a touch of honey. He was an expert on apitherapy, giving demonstrations on how to make the bees sting a person for medical purposes. He developed a method of collecting bee venom and was selling it in France. His visit to us was most significant though because he talked Don out of using deep supers for honey production. I guess Don just wanted to prove to himself that he could do it with all that heavy lifting. He used the deeps for nineteen years, from 1973 to 1992. But after he got all the shallows built for honey production, he was very grateful for Charlie Mraz's persuasive advice. This was from his visit ten years earlier. But in 2002, Don was truly thankful that he was dealing with shallow honey supers in the extracting room. Extracting was a job he always did solo.

By the time June rolled around, he felt like helping me in the garden, actually weedeating, raking, and mulching between my rows of flowers. We celebrated his seventieth birthday that June—so thankful that God was renewing his strength. I fixed a special birthday dinner for him, inviting some special friends to join us. We laughed at the birthday cake with a cow on it. He thought a lot about cows those days since he was given a cow's valve in his open-heart surgery. After dinner, we gathered in the living room to see the surprise video I had planned and secretly organized. It was so special, telling the story of our own Mech Apiaries, from 1973 to 2002. Included was a poem the Lord had given to me at three o'clock in the morning:

Thanks be to God for honeybees,
for friends and flowers and mountain breeze,
for honest work—a dream fulfilled.
A country life. We paid the bills!
For food to eat, enough to spare.
Our honey traveled everywhere,
from down the Pike, across the land.
The sweetness spread from bees to man.
And candles glowed when it was dark
from golden beeswax on the hearth.

In August 2002, I was blessed to have Brenda DuMont join me at the ninety-fifth anniversary of Pike Place Market. We set up a beautiful table with a special birthday "cake" made by Becky Town of the Dough Shop in Maple Valley. We won the grand prize and had a fun day.

Throughout the summer, Don continued to travel back and forth between the beeyards near Mount Rainier and Eastern Washington, doing his beekeeping work but just hiring a fellow to help when it was time for heavy lifting. In November, we had a nice dinner party for Bruno and Brigitte Lintz and Frank and Susan Fitzpatrick. Frank brought us several molds for candle making that he had found at a garage sale. I was so excited to get started making more candles again, but Don was dragging his feet, worrying that it would be too much—that we might spill the hot wax, get burned, or set the honey house on fire.

Well, I just gradually got all the candle molds out, including the ones Frank had given us. I put the wicking in each mold and clamped them down in their stands ready to pour. "Guess what," I said. "The molds are all ready for some hot beeswax to pour."

"Well, okay. I'll get the cardboard taped down to the floor and see what I can do." He was worried about doing this, but with the good Lord's help, we made a lot of beeswax candles.

About halfway through, four or five days into the project, our friends Frank and Susan Fitzpatrick drove up with a couple of boxes full of absolutely the most marvelous candle molds from Germany. We were thrilled. "You can use our molds. Those are our collection from when we lived in Germany."

This was truly wonderful. We borrowed them in subsequent years to come—so thankful for those wonderful friends. And so thrilled to see each beautiful candle as I took it out of the mold. And *yes*, we did not have a spill of hot beeswax nor did we burn the honey house down. Thanks be to God!

CHAPTER 14

The Good, the Bad, and the Ugly

THE WONDERFUL HONEY OF MECH APIARIES

Please don't throw rocks at the bees — They are just making honey

*I*t was remarkable that Don's new heart valve produced the desired effects. The doctors estimated it would give him eight more years of productive life. He was able to regain strength and carry on with the love and passion of his life, beekeeping. But many challenges came our way. The winds of adversity could have easily blown us off our feet had it not been for Christ, the solid rock on whose help I daily relied. I was gradually forced to deal with things beyond my comfort zone.

Living on five acres in the country holds challenges. I will never forget December 4 in 2003. The wind blew eighty miles per hour. Branches were flying through the air and trees falling to the ground right and left. Thank God, no trees hit our house, honey house, or propane tank. But there were at least six trees down, providing us with plenty of firewood to keep the home fires burning. God sent us so many different wonderful friends with chainsaws and strong muscles to help. We got all the debris carried into brush piles to burn in the spring when it dried out.

There were major ice storms that caused incredible damage to the trees too. More than once, I vividly remember hearing the cracking sound of trees that were breaking under the weight of icy limbs and sometimes a loud explosive crash as a tree fell onto the icy, snowy ground. It was beautiful to look at—like a lovely picture scene on a Christmas card—but what a lot of hard work, keeping things well taken care of on five acres. And there were so many times that the electricity would go out during a storm as well. But we learned to get by, planning ahead and filling buckets with water when a storm was predicted.

There was no running water, of course, when the power was out because our well water was pumped from the ground by electricity. We were warm enough with our wooly long johns on and a cozy fire burning in our coal-and-wood-burning stove in the living room.

The other rooms, such as Don's office and the master bedroom, were a different story. They were so cold that crusts of ice would turn the windows into works of graphic design. I could not persuade him to turn the propane furnace on.

"Oh no, we don't want our money going up the chimney," he'd say. His mind was set. He had to rule the roost.

"Was he easy to live with?" No! "How did you ever manage?" you may be asking, my dear reader.

There is one truth I sincerely wish I could pass on to you. If I can do it, so can you. You can put up with a lot of momentary unpleasant stuff *if* you keep your eyes on the Savior, the Lord Jesus. Keep looking up to him. Daily keep in touch. He speaks to you in his Word, the Bible. And the still, small voice of his Holy Spirit will guide you and give you peace. And the God of this universe hears your prayers in Jesus's name.

In 2009, the power was out for several days, and the temperature dropped to single-digit figures. Some pipes froze, and in the honey house, the toilet bowl was a block of ice. But we savored the heat from our Glacier Bay wood-and-coal burning stove on those cold, cold days and nights, and we were pleasantly nourished by the stews and soups that simmered slowly on top.

In my mind's eye, I can still smell the scarlet runner beans slowly cooking with Trader Joe's chicken apple sausage and diced apples from our orchard. I'd usually throw in a sweet onion from the cellar too and, of course, always a touch of honey. Down in the meadow, in the snow, the honeybees had their own way of keeping it warm inside each beehive. They clustered together tightly. The colder it was, the tighter their cluster. They took turns moving around so the same worker "girls" never had to be on the outside of the cluster too long. It was cold out there. In the very center of the cluster, there was always the queen bee—the lifeblood of the colony. They kept the temperature around seventy degrees for her, just with their own body heat, even though it might have been only twenty-five degrees outside. Life was basically good. The good, the bad, and the ugly all blended together as the pieces in a patchwork quilt.

A letter dated October 19, 2009, gives just a glimpse of life on the farm at Mech Apiaries in these days:

Dear Mom,

It's a dark, rainy Saturday. "The day was cold and dark and dreary. It rained and the wind was never weary."

I woke up at my regular time for Saturday, 5:30 a.m. Not strange, I guess, since I've been doing exactly that for thirty-seven years now.

And by now, 9:30 a.m., I would have our table all set up with honey, beeswax candles, and flowers.

The last two Saturdays were wonderful. I had enough to sell for a bountiful display, complete with autumn flowers and red leaves. And best of all, I had a very special dear helper, Brenda. She's a joy to be around and so helpful. Well, that is history now. There is not enough honey in the jars to go, sad. It's just sitting there in the honey house in five-gallon buckets waiting for someone who has the strength to take the lids off, lift it in the warming tank and then the bottling tank, and then put it in the jars.

It would be so nice to hire someone to help out, but Don is not interested in having anyone else around. For the last two days, he's been completely out of it with back pain, sleeping mostly, with some powerful pain pills. I was surprised that he did get the wood fire going this morning…

Then later on October 29:

Dear Mom,

A joyful day to you. "The joy of the Lord is in your strength" and "Weeping may endure for a night, but joy cometh in the morning."

Well, today is finally a day I've been waiting for. Don is back in the honey house. He is attempting to spend the day labelling jars and, after that, to bottle up some more honey. We'll see how it goes—one day at a time.

There are some buckets of huckleberry honey from 2004 and fireweed honey from 2003 that are still wonderful honey. Then there are some buckets of raspberry honey and maple blossom honey that we got from another local beekeeper. If we can manage to get it in the jars, I'll go to the market again—hopefully for holiday sales. My teenage helpers are praying for us and anticipating another day to work with me at the market. They are all such wonderful young people; there's Diane, Kim, Kelsey, Alyssa, Michael, Jacob, and also Brenda, who's not a teenager anymore but still likes to help me.

I am so blessed. God is good. He supplies all our needs according to his riches in glory by Christ Jesus, *right?*

November 30, 2009

Dear Mom,

Here it is, the last day of November. Now the Christmas countdown begins. Wow.

And that's not all. Saturday was *so* fun at the market. Michael helped me. A very amazing thing happened. A couple from Florida came all the way to Seattle *mostly* to get some of our honey. They had phoned me earlier, and I told them we were in retirement mode—not able to ship anymore and the only way they could get more was to see me on a Saturday at Pike Place. So here they were! Their adorable beagle had also made the flight. They asked to have a picture taken with me, so Michael volunteered. Just as he was snapping the picture, the beagle reached over and gave me a kiss. The lady was holding him in her arms. They were so happy. They had brought along an extra suitcase full of Bubble Wrap just for carrying our honey back to Florida. Isn't that amazing?

Amazing beyond words. Our heavenly Father *does* watch over his children. Just like the words of the song I sang so many times over the years: "And come what may, from day to day, my heavenly Father watches over me." And also, another song that comes to mind is equally true: "Through it all, through it all, I've learned to trust in Jesus. I've learned to trust in God. Through it all, through it all, I've learned to depend upon his Word."

I cannot recall the exact date of the following incident, but it will forever be in my memory. It was a stormy, cold winter Saturday at Pike Place Market in the busy days of brisk preholiday sales. We sold a lot of honey—honey in our pretty hexagon jars, honey packed in attractive gift boxes, honey still in the comb, honey fit for a king. Beeswax candles were a big attraction too. Their heavenly aroma made our space there so special—even divine. It was a thrill just to be there, in the midst of such beauty, and then to speak one by one to all the wonderful customers God sent our way.

If there was an occasional lull in business, I was so happy to speak with the farmers set up right next to me. They were the Webers from Cashmere, who came with mouthwatering crispy apples from their orchard on the other side of the mountains. We were running late at the end of the day, getting things all packed up and inventorying carefully in the process. The customers just kept coming. Closing time was six o'clock. Most of the other tables were bare. The farmers and craftspeople had already gone home. That's when I realized our cashbox was missing. I felt like someone had punched me really hard in the stomach. I couldn't believe this had happened. I actually was shaking so hard through my tears. I don't remember now who my teenage helper was that day, but I do distinctly remember the Webers, who were also late in packing up.

"I can't go home, Ingrid," I said. "I can't go home. I don't know what to do. Don will hit the roof in rage. I can't go home," I cried.

She hugged me then and said, "Can we help you? Let me talk to Tim."

"Okay," they said, "if you will follow us to the Union Gospel Mission where we're going to drop off our unsold apples, we will follow you home. We'll have dinner together and trust the Lord to see you through this."

At the dinner table, I told Don what had happened. His face turned white as a sheet, but there were no cruel, uncontrolled words. The telephone rang. It was the Pike Place Market Security. They had recovered our cashbox in a dumpster. The cash was gone, but all the checks written that day were still there. It was not a total loss. I offered to let the Webers sleep on our hide-a-bed before the long drive across the mountains. They gratefully accepted. But when we awakened the next morning, they were gone, quietly slipping away in the wee hours of the morning.

God had seen us through. All praise to him. He is so good.

This chapter is about the good, the bad, and the ugly, right? So now it is time to mention the truly ugly. I'd like to forget that ugly things ever came our way, but again God was there, even in the midst of it.

One sunny summer day, Don took off in his Chevy S-10 pickup to check on the beeyard above the town of Orting.

The fireweed flowers were in full bloom as far as you could see across the logged-off slopes of the mountain. Would the bees be needing more space to store the honey they were making from fireweed flowers? He was prepared. Extra shallow supers were loaded on the back of the truck. A tasty lunch was packed too for a nourishing break from all the work that lay ahead on that lovely day. This was really his dream job—working with the bees and bringing in a marvelous food that people highly treasured.

But as he drove up to the apiary, he could not believe what his eyes were seeing. The beehives were smashed to "smithereens." Only a couple were left standing out of a twenty-five-hive apiary. He stood on the ground aghast, wondering why, why, why would someone do such a terrible thing. He saw big tire tracks and a license plate on the ground. He saw the fencing wire wrapped round and round all twisted up, like it had been wrapped around the axle of the truck. There were deep marks in the soil where the truck had left in a hurry. "Good," he thought, "I hope they got stung up really bad when they had to stop to remove the fencing wire from their axle."

But why, why would someone do this to the honeybees? They were only gathering honey. He was dumbfounded, paralyzed by anger. He couldn't stand there and look at the disaster for another minute, so he headed back down the logging road.

On the way back down the mountain, he ran into a law enforcement officer. He showed him the license plate and told him what had happened.

"I'm so sorry," the officer said. "We've had a lot of trouble up here—drugs and firearms. We are swamped with cases, but I can give you a case number. I'll give you a call if we come up with anything."

That was it. In a very stunned frame of mind, he drove back home.

I hardly recognized him as my husband, as he walked through the door into our home. The whites of his eyes were totally bloodshot, and white foam was coming out of the corners of his mouth.

"This is it!" he screamed at the top of his voice. "It's all over!"

"Wait a minute, calm down," I said. "Tell me what happened."

"The bees are destroyed."

"It's a disaster!" he yelled. "You can't even believe what happened: total destruction. I can't face it. I can never go back there again. They can just stay in the mountains and rot into the hillside. I'm finished. I want out of here. Let's just get a divorce."

There was no calming down for him. I grabbed my purse, cell phone, and jacket and headed out the door into my van. I drove down the highway, crying out to the Lord for his mercy and his help. I parked close to the Cedar River Trail where I could go on my speed walk, breathe deeply, and listen to the loving, still, small voice of my heavenly Father.

"Fear not, I am with you," he said, "I will never leave you or forsake you."

I could breathe normally again when I returned to my van. I called my dear trusted friend, Brigitte, and told her what had happened. And I also called my precious aged mother who was a prayer warrior.

I drove back home and went ahead and began fixing our dinner.

The telephone rang, and it was Bruno, Brigitte's husband. "Hey, Don," he said. "I heard what happened today. I'm really sorry. I've been thinking I'd like to go with you—back up to the mountains—and help you clean up the disaster with your bees. Maybe there is a little left that I can help you salvage."

We ate dinner together then that evening, so grateful and amazed that our friend Bruno had volunteered to help out. A friend in need is a friend indeed. We were able to pick up the pieces and carry on. Thanks be to God.

The law enforcement officer did give us a call a few days later. From the license plate, they were able to find the owner of the truck, a single young man who still lived with his mother. The officer talked with the mother since her son was not home.

"Well, doesn't the beekeeper have any insurance?" was all she could say.

We never heard anything further on the case. So sad the way this world has become: people no longer caring and respecting one another and people choosing to walk in darkness and thinking only of themselves and a momentary high—forgetting to think before acting.

Amazingly, I still remember the simple happy days of my childhood. There was no lock on our door back in the thirties.

And even in 2001, twenty years ago from this day, there were amazing selfless, thoughtful young people that we were blessed beyond words to know, Brandon H., for example.

When Don's Mazda mini pickup work truck was totaled on a summer day in 2001, he was suddenly left with no way to take care of all the bees in the midst of their busiest harvest season. I checked around with all the possible car dealers in our area. Our needs were very specific. It had to be a mini-sized pickup to fit through the custom overhead door of our honey house. And Don said, "It has to be a stick shift too. I wanna be in charge!"

Several dealers were searching for our needs.

But in the meantime, Brandon said, "You know what, Mr. Mech, you can use my little truck. I can get by. I can ride to work with my neighbor. He works in the same shop. You can use it as long as needed."

We were blown away. Here was a nineteen-year-old young man letting us use his truck. We gratefully accepted his generous offer, and the honey harvest happened again that year.

CHAPTER 15

Treasures in the Bung Box

*I*t had been an unusually hot summer in 2009, with several days of temperatures over one hundred degrees. The grass, which had not been mowed down since last spring, was a wearisome two feet high. I convinced Don that it would be a good idea to get out the Weed eater and cut it down, especially in the center of the driveway, where sparks from the big GMC truck could start a fire. Here is an excerpt from a letter written:

July 25, 2009

Dear Mom,

It's a busy Saturday morning here at Mech Apiaries. After an early breakfast of French toast topped with fresh blueberries from the garden and coffee, Don started up the Weed eater. He mowed down the dry grass around the house and in the middle of the driveway. I was worried that he might fall on the uneven ground, but he was okay. Thanks be to God!

There is another beekeeper, a hobbyist, coming to look at Don's bee truck later today. At this point, he hates to part with it, but it's a hassle just to get it out on the road once a month to drive so it stays in shape. He hasn't moved bees with it since 2004, and I'm sure he won't be getting more hives.

We'll just take one day at a time, trusting in the Word's guidance—our good shepherd's voice.

Patricia Gentry, the beekeeper, was happy to buy our truck. She lived on Bainbridge Island—a great place to keep bees. She traveled back and forth on the ferry to come to the mainland, with a ferry pass, but a surprise awaited her on her way back home from Maple Valley. The boom on the truck was so tall that she had to pay an extra forty-six dollars to get it home across the Puget Sound. They wouldn't take the bee truck across the sound with her ferry pass. Before we let her drive the truck down the driveway, we carefully removed all our private items: the sleeping bag behind the seat, the tools and smoker in the custom-made metal box welded under the flatbed, and, of course, the treasures in the bung box.

The "bung box" is really another quite amusing name for the glove compartment under the dashboard. We first heard this term used back in 1964 when we were on vacation. We flew a little Cessna airplane all the way back to Illinois to visit Don's family. He was the pilot, and I was the navigator, watching maps to help keep us on course. We landed at a very small airstrip to eat dinner and then get a motel for the night. On the airstrip was a little neat building only about twelve feet by twelve feet. There was just a plain white table inside and two matching chairs. On the wall was a pegboard with keys hanging and a sign that read: "Dear visitor, please feel free to use the car parked outside if you'd like to drive into town. We have a good motel and a restaurant two miles up the road. Just leave the keys in the bung box when you come back. Thank you. Come again." We were so impressed with that genuine hospitality and trust. We were in the middle of farm fields—no houses in sight. It was either Nebraska or South Dakota. I don't remember which state, but we have never forgotten the "bung box" term. And by the way, it's not even in the dictionary.

Anyway, the treasures I rescued from the bung box that day in 2009 were two different little books that Don, the meticulous electrical engineer beekeeper, had kept. I was not even aware that he was writing down these detailed records. One was a notebook telling every time he moved a truckload of beehives. Here is one example from the year 1988:

> May 4 and 5: Moved 38 hives from Ronberg to Kalley. Madrona in bloom. Huckleberry is just starting.
>
> May 6 and 7: Moved 38 hives from Jelsma to Schillingers. Huckleberry in bloom. Also trailing blackberries.
>
> May 10 and 11: Moved 38 hives from Bussard to Jacobson in the first eighty degrees of the year.
>
> May 11 and 12: Moved 37 hives from Cooper to Gudger. Hot work!
>
> May 13 and 14: Moved 40 hives from Marenakos to Williams. Huckleberries near peak bloom. Late again!

June 22, 23, and 24: Moved 41 hives from Williams to Jacobs (boom failure, two trips.

June 28 and 29: Moved 41 hives from Jacobsen to Clark with a new winch. Reel is still a problem. Rod James helped.

July 1 and 2: Moved 40 hives from Kalley to Gale Creek in the *rain*. Fireweed is just starting to bloom.

July 7 and 8: Moved 40 hives from Schillingers to Sunset in nice weather. Boom *real* problem, getting worse.)

July 11 and 2: Moved 36 hives from Gudger to Emmerick. Knapweed is just starting to bloom. Boom working better.

July 27 and 28: Moved 41 hives from Jacobs to Camp Creek. Flat before loading! Kent helped unload. Doris helped load.

July 28 and 29: Moved 42 hives from home and Ronberg to Tacoma Creek. Doris helped load.

August 7 and 8: Moved 39 hives from Sunset Lake to Dyke's. Cool but clear weather. Doris helped load.

August 13 and 14: Moved 37 hives from Gale Creek to Camp Creek number 2 in cool cloudy weather.

September 26: Moved 34 hives from Tanum to Ronberg. Dave Noonan helped. New reel works great. Anthill!

September 28 and 29: Moved 41 hives from Tacoma Creek to Bussard's in start of nice weather.

September 30 and October 1: Moved 35 hives from Camp Creek number 2 to Cooper's in warm weather.

October 1 and 2: Moved 39 hives from Camp Creek number 1 to Jelsma's in beautiful weather.

October 4 and 5: Moved 38 hives from Clark to Ronberg. Flat on left front tire at house overnight!

October 5 and 6: Moved 38 hives from Dyke's to Marenokas. Went in the winter with 226 hives.

That piece of information from Don's notebook tells us that he loaded up our beehives on the big GMC one-ton flatbed twenty times in 1988. For twenty nights, he slept in that truck. At the drop of a hat, he would tell me, "We've got to get the bees moved to where the honey is coming in." I would swing into high gear and get two lunches and a breakfast packed into the cooler and, of course, a big thermos of Colombian roast coffee—his favorite.

Sometimes there were less bees to move out of an apiary than the ones we had originally trucked in. This was due to vandalism, theft, or disease. But in the eighties, times were good. We usually gained more hives because the bees were so healthy they swarmed, and we were able to catch a good number of the swarms and start new colonies. There was also the hope that if we split a strong hive, we could prevent swarming. This was another way we increased our hive count. But there was much more work to do involving that big truck than just moving the bees. There was also the honey crop to take off. But generally that was not an overnight affair.

"You know what?" Don mused as we were getting ready to part with that trusty old red truck. "I bet I have spent over a year of nights sleeping inside that truck with the bees loaded up on the flatbed."

"Wow! That would be 365 nights," I said. "Shall we just say— you sure worked hard?"

Yes. He did. Hard work never hurt anybody, and he loved it. Only now, after really taking a good look at his meticulous notebook did I calculate it was over 600 nights. Many starry nights with the Big Dipper clearly in view and all the constellations. Stars without number and northern lights as well in the clear open skies beyond city lights.

There was another small very worn notebook that only another beekeeper would appreciate. It was covered with propolis—that very sticky substance that bees gather from buds of trees. In it were detailed records of the status of every beehive back in the seventies. Was the queen doing her job? It told of the health and well-being of a particular hive for up to five years or until it died out or was united with another colony. Here's an example of his record keeping:

Hive number 111
July 7, 1975: Hive swarmed at Quackenbush (low branch)

July 13, 1975: QR
July 6, 1976: Swarmed and made three nucs, left two QCs
June 14, 1976: 1 QC hat, 1 QC capped
June 19, 1976: No QCs, no Es, gave three QCs on FR
June 27, 1976: 1 chewed QC
July 5, 1976: Es—Q
July 25, 1976: QR
May 8, 1977: SUP—Gave HWQ NUC
May 19, 1977: No Es Qs
May 20, 1977: Left 1 QC—2 BRD FR
June 2, 1977: 1 Hat'd 1 NEW QC
June 13, 1977: E's and LAR
May 20, 1978: Cut QCs
June 20, 1978: Swarmed—NO BRD
June 27, 1978: Es and LAR

I realize that these words, to most people, would be like finding hieroglyphics. To me also, they are partially beyond understanding. I can tell you that QR means queenright, QC would be queen cells,

SUP would be super, E would be eggs, BRD would be brood. The rest is a mystery to me.

In that one little book, he was keeping track of 180 beehives. He periodically checked them all to know the condition of each beehive. It broke his heart to have to shake the bees out on the ground and take away their home, but this is exactly what had to be done if a hive became a drone-laying hive. That meant it had become queen-less and the worker bees were desperate. They laid eggs, but their eggs were unfertile, and they only developed into drones.

The queen was truly the lifeline of the hive. If she began to fail and not keep up her task of laying around two thousand eggs a day, she would be wiped out by the beekeeper. Then given a new queen, which might be shipped in from California or Hawaii. Or he might just choose to let the bees raise their own new queen from queen cells from another strong colony. There were many different views on this topic and many helpful articles to read in the beekeeping magazines: *American Bee Journal* and *Gleanings in Bee Culture*. That was his evening pastime, reading current articles on beekeeping in front of a crackling fire.

So what did you think? Did I find a treasure? Did I find something valuable that was hidden away in darkness? Obviously, it was not of such amazing historical significance as the Bayeux Tapestry made in the eleventh century, still on view in a museum in northern France. Nor does it even come close to my father's schoolbooks being uncovered between the walls of the one-hundred-year-old Pearson farmhouse. Hidden treasures are wonderful. Finding them is exciting. Maybe someday, a hundred years from now, someone will wonder how did one man make a living with honeybees—working endlessly, mostly all alone—tucked away on five acres in the midst of King County and over two million people.

CHAPTER 16

Discovered

*O*ver the years, it has been so absolutely amazing how the wonderful honey produced by our bees was discovered and highly appreciated. Not once did it ever enter our minds to hire a marketing strategist. But good news and especially good news about good food does travel. There was no doubt that the Lord was blessing us. "We know that every good and every perfect gift is from above and cometh down from the Father of Lights, with Whom is no variableness, neither shadow of turning" (James 1:17).

In 1985, we were on the cover of *American Bee Journal*, a nationwide magazine for beekeepers. It showed our table at Pike Place Market on a summer day, beautifully arrayed with bouquets of flowers for sale amidst an orderly array of honey in jars and honey in wooden totes. We also wholesaled those totes to a place in Seattle-Tacoma International Airport.

We were blessed with such good exposure. Pike Place Market was and is a Seattle landmark and tourist destination for travelers nationwide and around the world.

In the eighties and nineties, we were going to the market about one hundred days a year. People loved our honey. It was a joy to see customers return again and again. Back at home on the farm, our telephone would ring quite regularly with a friendly voice enquiring how to get another jar. Our answering machine played a little from the "Flight of the Bumblebee" before my message: "Things are really buzzing around here. Sorry we missed you. Leave your name and number and we will buzz you back."

Post office box 452 also was often filled with letters from people across America who had picked up a small jar of our honey while on vacation and visiting the Pike Place Market. They all said pretty much the same thing: "The honey we got from you was so delicious. There is nothing like it where we live. Could you please send info on how we can order more by mail?"

This was another one of my tasks. I was well-known at the Maple Valley Post Office. When I had heavy boxes to ship, I always waited until a young guy pulled up in the parking lot and asked him if he might help me bring the boxes into the post office. I always brought along a honey bear or a piece of honeycomb to say thanks. People were so nice to help the "Honey Lady."

In September of 1992, I was making way more trips to the post office than usual. The *Country Woman* magazine had a little story about Mech Apiaries in Maple Valley. The letters flooded into our mailbox from Tennessee to Vermont and everywhere in between. And then, of course, the orders for honey followed. It was a joyous experience. The Lord knew beforehand that we needed a lift. The *Country Woman* story was published in September, and my father died of a sudden massive heart attack in August. My heavenly Father cared so much for me then as he does now and every day.

The following year, in 1993, I received an invitation to be a guest speaker on a radio station, WBCL, in Fort Wayne, Indiana. It was a call-in talk show with Char Binkley. The program was called *What's Cookin'*. With modern technology, I got to sit at my own kitchen desk and talk to people all over Indiana. I loved it. More honey orders came in as well as orders for the second edition of my book *Joy with Honey* which was published that year.

Right here at home in the greater Seattle area, I was also privileged to be a guest on the KIRO radio studio with the honorable Jim French. His in-depth interviews with authors and speakers covered a broad spectrum of knowledge and was very popular in the days when so many people got their news, information, and entertainment from the radio. Slowly, we were being discovered.

The Seattle Times featured another story about Mech Apiaries on October 9, 1991. We were operating around 250 beehives then, but beekeeping was beginning to get quite challenging. Many factors—including urban sprawl, overuse of pesticides, vandalism, and parasitic mites—were resulting in the die-off of honeybee colonies. We still chose to stick with our peaceful passion—the practice of beekeeping. Somehow, by the help of God—*by faith and a spin*—we were able to keep going. Our hive count gradually diminished down to around 100 hives. We were glad to have a large inventory of honey stored in five-gallon buckets from the good years. Honey does not spoil. It usually crystallizes but can easily be reliquefied at low temperatures. It is a well-known fact that pure delicious honey was discovered in Egypt in King Tut's tomb. The honey was sealed in pottery and in perfectly good condition after more than two thousand years.

So our honey supply lasted as long as needed, and more people discovered how delicious it was.

One day in the late eighties, two young men from California stopped by our honey stand at Pike Place Market. They were brothers, I believe, the Corti Brothers to be exact. They knew and appreciated fine food. They were masters of discovery. They were owners of the Corti Brothers, a gourmet grocery in Sacramento.

The Corti family has been in business since 1947. They are a prominent name in the food industry—highly respected for their skill in finding everything from the finest wines, olive oil, mushrooms, and tea, to name a few. They travel the world literally and meet the producers from Greece to Córdoba, Spain; Japan; China; New Zealand; Australia; and, of course, Italy. They search America too—for the finest food and wine. Darrel Corti is an amazing gold mine of information on fine food and wines. By now, you must have guessed that they discovered our honey. You are right. Their first discovery that came to our attention was with our most unique maple blossom honey. They began serving it, paired with Gorgonzola cheese as a dessert at their gala VIP dinner. We began shipping it by the case to Sacramento. Their appreciation and enthusiasm for our varietal honeys was heartwarming.

They called it "exquisite." Blackberry blossom, raspberry blossom, wild huckleberry, Mount Rainier fireweed, in addition to our unique honey of the spring, maple blossom. They offered these for quite some time.

Then in 2000, our bees produced another unique honey in the month of July. It was an unusual year. The ground was saturated with abundant rain, followed by a hot sunny spell. Everything in the meadow on our farm came into bloom at the same time. There was wild blackberry, wild cucumber or man-in-the-ground growing on top of the blackberries, white clover, and snowberry along the edge of the woods. The honey had a delicious light flavor. I like the way Darrel Corti described it as follows:

> Labeled "meadow," it has just been extracted from the combs and has a pale yellow, slightly green tinged, almost transparent color. The scent is delicate, flowery but not specific, with a fresh, light flavor. It is very flavory but not overpoweringly "honey-like" nor fatiguing. In fact, it is very much the honey equivalent of some of the botrytized wines made from grape varieties, such as Chenin blanc or Riesling. The finish is very

clean, balanced, and delicate. It would make an excellent accompaniment to fried foods as a dipping sauce together with a bit of our Puree de Piment d'Espelette for contrast.

That was twenty-one years ago.

In January 2020, I picked up my cell phone and, on a whim, dialed his number. Miracle of miracles, he was at his desk, not traveling the world in search of the finest food. He remembered Mech Apiaries. Yes, he did. We had a cordial conversation, and I was "lost" in wonder and amazement.

Discovered indeed! We got word that they were talking about our meadow honey in New York City on WCBS Newsradio. Then it was written up in the food section of *Vogue* magazine in December 1991.

Good news does travel. Martha Stewart had her staff call us next, to see if we'd be willing to wholesale our honey. She wanted to put her own label on it. Seriously. We were very much honored, but we declined her offer. Our label would stay with the honey that our bees produced.

A couple of years later in 1995, when I was selling our honey and beeswax candles at the Pike Place Market, a lady walked up to our stand and introduced herself as Linda Eckhardt. "I have something I'd like to give you," she said. She handed me a hardbound book she had recently written. It was titled *Linda Eckhardt's 1995 Guide to America's Best Foods*. We were written up on page 50 as "Epicure's Honey." She had obviously loved our honey, but I had completely forgotten our earlier interview. There were tears in my eyes as I sincerely thanked her for this compliment. And there were more letters in post office box 452 as well.

Discovery goes both ways. Have you ever thought about that? It's such a good feeling to be discovered and appreciated by others for some deed you have done in the past. It doesn't have to be something grand and magnificent, although it can be. A simple act of kindness, a small token of gratitude, a smile, or a seed planted that later bursts into bloom are all like rippling happy memories. Remembering and discovering them again is a heartwarming source of delight, as this letter, which was written to my mother when she was ninety-one:

August 14, 2003, 9 a.m.

Dear Mom,

How are you today?

As I write this letter, I am giving my feet a luxury treatment. I'm soaking them in a mixture of warm oil and *honey*. Sure feels good. I'm hoping it will heal the calluses. A couple of spots were getting sore.

I just talked to a man from Albuquerque, New Mexico, who bought our honey from Pike Place Market several years ago. I had given him and his wife a little beeswax ornament. He said I probably didn't realize that I was very much a part of their family because, every year, they took the beeswax ornament out and put it on their Christmas tree, and they thought of their trip to Seattle and our honey. And I quote: "The very best honey in the world." What a nice compliment! Now that gives me the idea to start giving away beeswax ornaments to our good honey customers. I've only done it occasionally in the past.

Now my feet feel refreshed. I'm going out to the garden to pick some flowers.

Love,
Doris and Don

CHAPTER 17

A Busy Beekeeper's Year

When most people think of beekeeping as a profession, they tend to look at it as quite a simple, uncomplicated occupation. After all, don't the bees do all the work? You just go and rob them of all the honey they've made. You have plenty of spare time to do whatever your heart desires. I've heard that more than once. To those unaware, let me tell you just a few things that filled our calendar during years of peak production, in the eighties and nineties when we were operating with around 250 beehives.

January
Take an inventory of everything in the honey house.
Work on income taxes, state and federal.
Check electric fences in the apiaries.
Check for signs of skunks, mice, and ants.
Workshop time—repair and build new equipment

February
Get boxes set up for comb honey production.
Keep labelling jars and filling them with honey to sell at the farmer's market and wholesale to stores.
Go and buy a truckload of jars and don't forget the lids.
Unload with a hand truck and stack in neat rows in the honey house.

March
Medicate for American foulbrood.
Check the weight of hives and feed the light ones.
Make sugar syrup.
Remove deadouts from the apiary.
Clean up that equipment.
Repaint weathered hives boxes, covers, and bottom boards.

April
Dandelions in bloom.
Put pollen traps on in local apiaries.
Queens arrive in the mail.
Split hives and introduce the royal ladies.
Strong hives should have a crop of maple blossom honey beginning.

May
Harvest maple blossom honey.
Move hives to islands for huckleberry honey.
Swarm time.
Be looking and ready with extra supers and a tall ladder.
Extract maple honey and bottle some up for eager customers.

June
Harvest huckleberry honey.
Extract huckleberry honey—put some in jars and some in five-gallon buckets for huckleberry honey taffy.
Move bees to low-elevation mountain yards.

July
Blackberry honey flow.
Fireweed honey flow in low mountain elevations.
Harvest blackberry and raspberry honey.
Remove pollen traps—clean and store.
Move some hives to Eastern Washington for snowberry, knap-weed, alfalfa, and clover yards.
Gather up lots of "cow chips" for smoker fuel.
Use solar wax melter on sunny days.

August
Move bees to high mountain locations for fireweed honey.
Harvest fireweed honey by the end of August.
Keep electric fences intact to keep out bears. Pray that vandals stay away.
Extract the blackberry honey and put some in jars—gallon jars too because Dr. Hall wants three.
Clean bee pollen on a warm, dry day.

September
Harvest honeys made in Eastern Washington, keeping different apiaries marked—snowberry, alfalfa, clover, and knapweed.
Harvest fireweed honey.

Extract, label more jars, bottle up honey, and wash buckets.

September is National Honey Month.

Say yes if asked to give a talk. Bring the observation hive. And a couple of drone bees in your pocket, just for fun.

October

Finish extracting honey.

Roundup time.

Bring all the beehives home to local yards from Eastern Washington and the mountains.

Don't forget to change the oil and give the truck a lube job too.

Medicate all the hives.

Melt down beeswax cappings and make candles.

Feed light hives.

November

Make more candles. Clean up. Organize.

Label jars and honeycomb rounds.

Bottle up *a lot* of honey for holiday sales.

Go to the beekeepers' club annual potluck dinner and tall tales night.

Thanksgiving—count our blessings!

December

Check the apiaries after snow, ice, and wind storms.

Get out the long johns and sell honey, bee pollen, candles, and gift boxes at our open-air stand at Pike Place Market.

Enjoy Christmas with the family.

And, oh yes, help Doris ship out mail-order honey gift boxes at the post office to honey lovers across the country.

I have only touched the surface of a successful beekeeper's activities. Of utmost importance is to be on top of changing circumstances. New challenges arise inevitably, as sure as the changing seasons. We found it of utmost value to read the current beekeeping magazines which I mentioned earlier as well as keeping in touch with other beekeepers in our area. This too takes time, but it is time well spent.

Beekeeping was the core of our livelihood. But there was more work involved in keeping up our five acres. Like the incredibly wise King Solomon said in the third chapter of Ecclesiastes: "To every thing there is a season... A time to plant, and a time to pluck up that which is planted... A time to break down, and a time to build up... A time to cast away stones, and a time to gather stones together..."

In winter, there were frozen pipes to deal with, snow to be shoveled from our three-hundred-foot driveway, gutters to be cleared, overhead lights to be replaced, and *always* the home fires burning with coal and wood chopped from downed trees on the property.

Springtime brought a new flurry of activity. In addition to working with the bees, it was time to get the Troy-Bilt rototiller out. As soon as the ground was dried out enough, all the weeds needed to be tilled under. Some years, we planted cover crops, such as alfalfa or crimson clover, which grew in our area over the winter. Then in springtime, the soil was built up and enriched as we rototilled it back into the nice rich soil. Then we could begin planting our first crops into the garden—potatoes, peas, cabbage, broccoli, garlic, and onions. Every spring as we rototilled, we found more rocks in the soil. Many times, I remember following Don behind the rototiller with a five-gallon bucket picking up rocks. Don't worry, I only filled those buckets half full. They felt like a ton. We had a good use for them—filling potholes in our driveway.

Another springtime job was pruning all the fruit trees in our orchard. There were apple trees, pear trees, greengage, and Stanley plums, cherry, and Asian pears, my favorite. We bought a book that told how and when fruit trees should be pruned. All the branches pruned off had to be carried out and placed in a big burn pile. And every spring, we also had to prune back the evergreen and Himalayan blackberries that wanted to crowd out the orchard. We let them grow around the edge of the woods though because they were an excellent source of nectar for the bees the following July. And of course, we enjoyed eating them too—blackberry jelly, blackberry lemonade, blackberry muffins, blackberry pie, and more. But there has to be a limit set on those aggressive blackberry vines. More than once, they actually got away from us and grew all the way over the roof of our pump house.

Summertime was especially busy with the bees, but there were things to do on the farm too. Don purchased a sickle bar mower to keep the orchard mowed. We built fences around young fruit trees to keep the deer from eating the tender young leaves on low branches. And to further deter their nibbling, we sprinkled human hair around the edge of the fences. It was hair swept off the floor by our local barber. He was happy to help us out, and it really worked well for a couple of years. The deer were funny to watch, especially the little fawns. They would twitch their tails and leap away from the smell of human hair. I guess, after a couple of years, they finally decided that humans were harmless, at least on our farm. We loved watching them. There was plenty of good wild vegetation for them to eat in the woods and in the meadow. Our garden had a nice sturdy six-foot fence, and they never once jumped over. That we were aware of. The grass grew tall in the meadow with wild daisies growing amidst Scotch broom, evening primrose, and digitalis. Don mowed it all using his sickle bar mower and finished it off neatly using his Weed eater. He was never afraid of hard work, even after a long day of work in the apiaries. After the tall grass was mowed, we let it dry a day or two in the summer sunshine. Then came the task of raking it up in rows, all by hand, and then carrying it by pitchfork loads to make big haystacks. He enjoyed this a lot. It reminded him of his father who had been known to make the best haystacks in Cook County, Illinois. It was said they even shed the rainwater.

We didn't have farm animals, other than honeybees, to need all that hay, but we had a very good use for it. It made an excellent mulch for the garden. I had rows and rows of dahlias and perennials as well as strawberries, raspberries, blueberries, currants, tayberries, and Waldo blackberries. We mulched between every row, laying down the hay three or four inches deep on top of the soaker hoses. This kept the weeds from growing. And besides, it kept the moisture in the soil. We mulched the vegetable garden as well. I was the gardener, doing the planning, the planting, the dividing, the weeding, the pruning and deadheading, and the harvesting. Oh yes, I also had to deal with garden pests, like slugs, field mice, moles, and insects. As much as possible, we tried to garden organically, but that's another book. Don did help me with mole problems when he was able. Later, we had pretty good results with solar devices that we plunged into the ground which periodically emitted a high-pitched sound.

Rabbits were a major challenge some years. I finally was able to put up chicken wire all around the perimeter of the garden with the help of a dear friend, Karen Petch. Another summer job that Don usually attempted to do was get out his chain saw and cut firewood. In our woods, there were alders that grew amazingly fast, and there were tall firs that swayed in the wind right in the direction of our neighbors'—the Whites—house. When they mentioned their fear of a tree hitting their home, we didn't waste any time in taking those trees down. We had a good supply of firewood for a couple of years after that.

Summer days were bright and beautiful. When the temperatures rose to an uncomfortable degree, we were refreshed by cool air that gently drifted in from the woods on the hill behind our home. A big fan beside the open door was our mode of air-conditioning.

Olaf, our cat, thought that was a great setup. He could go in and out as he pleased and bring his latest catch into the house to show us. Sometimes it was alive and good for hours of cat and mouse games or sometimes ready for a freshly caught meal. Over the years, there were usually always cats in our lives: Olaf, Violet, Licorice, Button, Beau, and Catalina. Aslan, our unforgettable dog, was also an integral part of our lives in his life span. More later.

As you know, summer passes quickly, and before you know it, the slight coolness of fall is in the air. Autumn harvesttime comes and, with it, golden and red leaves announcing a new season has arrived. It's time to gather the harvest in from the garden. There are pumpkins and squash of every size, shape, and color. There are scarlet runner beans, dry in their long pods, to pull down from eight-foot-tall teepees. We'll store them away in the cellar for baked beans in the cold winter.

Work awaits in the orchard too. There are apples to pick. We get out the three-pronged orchard ladder and together carry it up to the orchard. Don climbs up to pick each apple as I hold the ladder steady. He places them in a bucket securely fastened to the ladder. Then I carefully transfer them into bushel boxes on the ground. There were *so* many apples. They had been well pollinated by our honeybees. We enjoyed them in every way imaginable, from crispy salads to autumn apple pork chops to the all-time favorite—apple pie.

One year, we also took several bushels of apples over to our friend Bob Quackenbush's place. He had a dandy cider press. That was the best cider I ever tasted, hot or cold. I can still remember that delicious mouthwatering treat—hot cider in mugs, with a touch of honey, a little grated ginger root, and cinnamon stick to stir.

Harvesting was work. But harvesting was also such a time of joy—gratefulness to God for the bounty we were blessed with. Then the leaves fell and blew through the air. Leaves from big-leaf maple, cottonwood, alder, silver maple, cascara, linden, wild hazelnut, and more. We had another big job that had to be done immediately: clean the roofs and gutters of both the honey house and our home. With all our lovely maple trees in Maple Valley, there was always a double gutter cleaning required. The leaves fell first. Then next, a couple of weeks later, the little twirly seeds fell, sailing through the sky like helicopters. They quickly filled up the clean gutters again, so up on the rooftops we went once more, hopefully able to blow the little seeds out with a handheld blower.

In the garden, there was plenty of cleanup work to do too. Mostly, I worked at that—digging and dividing all the dahlias and storing away the tubers in our cellar. From time to time, Don also helped in the garden—especially digging the potatoes. Spuds were one of his favorite foods, and he wanted to make sure there were lots of them.

Then after the sunflowers and cornstalks were carried away to a brush pile and the scarlet runner bean teepees were dismantled, the garden was rototilled again. Before rototilling in the fall, we liked to add compost from all our kitchen scraps and also several bags of human hair that the barber saved for us. We had read in a gardening magazine how hair was such a good fertilizer, slowly decomposing and adding nitrogen into the soil. Of course, the hay used for mulch earlier was also tilled right into the soil. It took three or four runs across the garden to do a good job, but the soil was lovely. Beautiful soil, in fact, without the pesticides added. We strived for organic gardening for over thirty years on that land. It was good.

CHAPTER 18

Retiring

Our retirement was quite unique, much unlike people in other occupations. Indeed, our whole career was unique. So why would retirement be anything different? Most retirees abandoned their five-days-per-week jobs quite abruptly with a fanfare celebration, possibly as a fellow farmer at Pike Place Market did. Doug and Clarissa Cross sailed around the world. Not us. Ours was a gradual process, slowly withdrawing from the hard physical work of beekeeping. We were blessed in many ways—being able to choose our own hours, having the honey house right beside our home, and avoiding a daily commute. But other things took up our time.

The circumstances that brought about our retirement were simply our aging bodies. In addition to a patched-up heart, Don began developing arthritis—severe pain in many joints of his body. This was relieved somewhat by medication and physical therapy as well as hot and cold treatments, but sitting in his La-Z-Boy recliner became the norm. His buddy Catalina gladly joined him, contentedly curled up on his lap.

The doctors were always amazed when they heard of Don's routine. Even up to his last day on the farm, he was able to get downstairs to where his exercise bike was. Our son-in-law Max had installed a second handrail on the stairwell which helped make the daily trek possible. Every day, he exercised on his bike for thirty minutes beside the window watching all the birds, squirrels, and other wildlife.

We treasured the fact that our property was registered as a wildlife refuge. He never wanted to leave. But gradually, we slowed down, as he was no longer really interested in the bees. We later only kept about twenty hives in our meadow—never moving them out for honey production. It was wonderful to have them there, pollinating our fruit trees in the spring. But the orchard was sadly one thing we could not maintain. After major ice storms, the trees were badly damaged. Blackberry vines then quickly took over.

A big black bear came and broke the center of my favorite Asian pear tree and one of the apple trees as well. Once, I actually saw him standing under the greengage plum tree in early summer. He looked up at all the plums hanging ripe on the branches. I could read his mind. Without any hesitation, I grabbed my big stainless steel bread-making bowl and a large spoon. I ran up the driveway toward the orchard where he was standing, making as much noise as I could, banging on the pan. It worked too. I scared him off into the woods. Then I didn't waste any time picking those sweet plums.

In our retirement years, gradually all the jobs of maintaining a five-acre farm had to be hired out. Some people were willing to barter for labor. We bartered firewood, dahlia tubers, honey, and even our Troy-Bilt rototiller and sickle bar mower, just to name a few. The work was still there, always waiting to be done, but now it was time to let others help. We were blessed with countless good people who came and offered assistance. Some we hired, but some came out of the goodness of their hearts—like Aaron's family. They came when our grass was dangerously high and dry in the summer. They just drove in— Aaron, his brother, his mom, and his dad—with mowers, Weed eaters, pruning shears, and gloves. They worked together for hours. We were so very grateful. We wanted them to come in and have a home-cooked meal, but they declined. They were there to work. It was an awesome sight. And when they were finished, it looked like a park.

I was having challenges with my health as well—heart issues. I couldn't seem to get it through my head that my body was no longer thirty years old. I enjoyed working hard in the garden and clearing pathways through the woods for exciting adventures, walks with our grandchildren. It felt good to work up a sweat, but my aging body didn't agree. It was time to slow down. Like a top that spins, our bodies are not designed to spin forever. Our slowdown was quite evident as shown on the following graph, telling how many days we spent selling at Pike Place Market each of the last fifteen years of our tenurial days there.

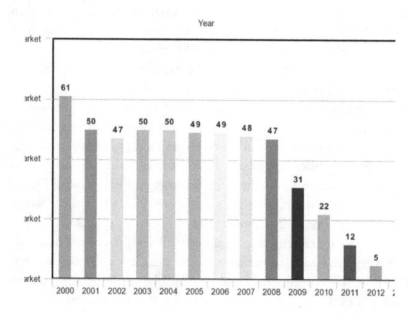

As we slowed down our frequency of going to the market, I was so thankful to have the garden. I spent hours and hours there, lost in dahlias, sweet peas, goldenrod, and globe thistle. It was my own wonderful private sanctuary, where I could tend God's lovely handiwork and listen to his still, small voice amidst the towering sunflowers and scarlet runner bean teepees. I could dream and plan. I could move a plant to wherever I thought it would look the most beautiful. I could create pathways and secret nooks for a cozy cup of ice tea with a friend. I could quietly sit under the rose arbor and watch the hummingbirds darting from the alstroemeria to the monarda. And I could marvel at all the different kinds of little bees that were pollinating our raspberries and blueberries.

There were bumblebees of different colors—black, white, yellow, and bright orange. They were big and fluffy. There were many different species of smaller bees as well. Bees that lived in the wild. We were so thankful we had a piece of land where nature could live with the changing seasons the way God planned it. Of course, there were the honeybees there in our garden as well. They had their favorites, and I grew anise hyssop, sedum, goldenrod, and Christmasberry just for them. I could also dream of music in the garden—the gentle sound of harps filling the air—amidst the twittering and singing of birds.

I mentioned this dream to a dear lifelong friend Gail McEwen. She had recently retired from a career as a music educator and then began taking harp lessons. Her sister Mary followed her lead, and soon a neighbor, Maria, joined her to form a harp trio. Their first concert was in my garden. We had a wonderful afternoon drinking lemonade, ice tea, and cookies. We sat under the shade of pop-up tents and dressed up with dresses and garden hats. Friends came from swim aerobics, from church, from BSF, and more. Family came too from far and wide. It was such a success that we did it again the next year. In fact, we celebrated Harps in the Garden for seven years in Maple Valley.

God knew I needed this beautiful garden in our retirement years. Don was a bear to live with. He had so many challenging health issues. In the year 2008, he had shingles, skin cancer, and a fractured wrist and hand from a fall. That in addition to appointments with hearing aid specialists, sleep apnea specialists, optometrists, and, don't forget, the dentist. He was just not able to do the work with the bees.

The twentysome hives that we had left were in our meadow. We were not able to truck them to different areas for making varietal honeys. And Don was not even capable of caring for them as he had done for so many years in the past. The apiary slowly dwindled down. We lost a couple of strong hives to swarming. Then one by one to colony collapse disorder. It was very depressing to Don to remove the deadouts from the apiary and then have the job of cleaning up that equipment. Those were dark days.

Here is a letter I wrote my mother in 2008:

October 17, 2008

Dear Mom,

This morning, I've been thinking of the song:

O give me a home
Where the buffalo roam,
Where the deer and the antelope play,
Where never is heard a discouraging word,
And the skies are not cloudy all day.

I am so tired of discouraging words! But I want to say thank you, Mom, for all your very encouraging, positive, upbuilding, cheerful words in our home when I was a child. I appreciate that so much now—especially when it seems so far-fetched these days.

But we must focus on Jesus—the author and finisher of our faith. May you have a blessed day—spreading sunshine.

Love,
Doris and Don

The last half-dozen hives in our apiary were sadly poisoned in an effort of our county to eradicate Japanese knotweed—a bush which grew prolifically on the banks of the Cedar River. It was an amazing source of nectar for the honeybees in the fall. The honey was delicious too, thick and very dark in color, such a contrast to the other light delicate honeys we produced in earlier years.

Amazingly, in the early years of our retirement, the bees sitting in the meadow produced a crop of honey for us every summer. Don was able to get supers on them, and when it was time to take the honey off, it was a *big* exciting day. He spent several days in advance in eager anticipation. The big bee truck would be awakened from its sleeping dock in the honey house and actually be driven for about two hundred feet down to the meadow. Its faithful boom, still running, picking up the heavy supers of honey and loading them up on the flatbed. He always asked for a helping hand in the final harvest.

For many years, it was Dima Banin who enjoyed giving him a hand in this process. They picked a sunny day, first using a fume board to encourage the worker bees to vacate the fresh combs of honey. The Bee-Go fumes smelled just like almonds—not at all bad to me, but the bees didn't like it. Most of them went back into the brood boxes or back to their work in the sunshine, gathering nectar and pollen from blooming flowers. They used a blower to get the remaining worker bees off the combs, lifting up each super just enough to blow the bees up into the air. Then quickly Dima would lift the super into the right position to be loaded up onto the flatbed. They had to work quickly, also making sure they didn't let the fresh honey be exposed. They placed special covers on the honey supers to prevent a robbing frenzy from other hives in the apiary. When they had gotten all the boxes neatly stacked on the back of the truck, they proceeded to tie the whole load down with manilla climbing rope— just the same way Don had done it for over three decades. Only this time, it was for a short trip back to the honey house—two hundred feet to be exact. It was a far cry from the many miles he had traveled with the bees in the good old days. But we were grateful to get a fresh new crop, however small, and also a few supers of comb honey that

I cut in small chunks to sell at the market. This was such a special treat—"nature's candy" as we called it.

My days of going to the market slowly decreased in our retirement years. We withdrew into the confinement of our farm, but our supply of honey and beeswax candles never ran out. The Lord truly supplied all our needs, just like he promised to do in 1 Peter 5:7. Five acres in Maple Valley, Washington, was a wonderful place to retire. We were always in awe of the beautiful wildlife right outside our door. There were birds and bees and creatures great and small.

One day, I was loading up my van with honey, pollen, and books to be delivered. It was parked at the loading dock on the east side of our honey house. Suddenly, I heard a chicken squawking very loudly. I know what chickens sound like when they are alarmed. When I was a child, I enjoyed watching the chickens at Grandma and Grandpa's house. But this chicken's voice was coming from the sky. I looked up, and only a few feet above my head was a bald eagle with a live chicken in its talons. No wonder that chicken was squawking.

I quickly ran into the honey house where Don was washing buckets in the extracting room. "You won't believe what I just saw," I said as I excitedly told him. "He was flying with a chicken in his grip, way up toward the top of the hill to the tallest fir tree."

"Run and get binoculars," he said.

We took turns, watching as two bald eagles had chicken dinner.

Another year, one of our neighbors' peacocks decided to come live on our place. What gloriously beautiful birds. This cock enjoyed strutting its feathers and seeing its own reflection in our honey house windows. I fed it cracked corn and frozen peas and sweet corn, thawed with hot running water. It was so tame that it actually ate out of Don's hand. And it enjoyed watching him work inside the honey house. It would sit on a sawhorse outside the extracting room window and watch what was going on. At night, it would roost way up high in a big-leaf maple tree in the edge of the woods.

Early one morning, as we were eating breakfast, we were startled to see him flying in circles around our house. And he was sounding very alarmed.

"Something's wrong," Don said. "I'll go see." He left half his breakfast on the plate and hurried over to the honey house.

I wish to this day that I had gone with him to see that amazing sight. A bobcat was sitting on the sawhorse which was the peacock's usual perch, and the peacock was on the roof of the honey house looking down. When the bobcat saw Don, he quickly jumped off the sawhorse and disappeared into the woods out of view.

We never knew what the next surprise would be—a lost young bull looking in the window or a mountain beaver in our basement. We were even greatly blessed to have one of America's rarest mammals nesting with their young in a box of kindling in our car port. We were cleaning things up one day and discovered they were there. There, right before our eyes, they made several trips, back and forth, carrying their young into the woods. They were black-footed ferrets.

And so we retired. Well, actually we went into retirement mode. We cut off all mail orders and deliveries to local outlets. There still was a decent supply of treasure from the bees, however. Like pure gold, it was still precious, special varietal honeys and pure golden beeswax candles. The honey lovers continued to seek us out. Out-of-state customers still wanted more. When they called on the telephone, we explained that in our retirement mode we were now exclusive at Pike Place Market. If they wanted more, they would need to have a friend or relative call us to see if we were able to be at our table on the following Saturday. Then they could pick up the honey or candles and mail them up. It was exciting to have such a treasured commodity and to interact with all our dear customers.

Don was pretty much out of the picture now. The last major laborious bottling run he made was in 2008. That was the year *Seattle Post-Intelligencer* came and did a story called "Feeling the Sting." And sadly, that was also the year that *Seattle Post-Intelligencer* folded its doors.

Our final day on the farm tables in the North Arcade of Pike Place Market was on a Saturday in 2014 just before Christmas. It was a banner day with Lisa Macdonald by my side. Saying goodbye to all our customers and wonderful market fellow farmers was not easy, but we still treasure all the memories of those amazing forty years.

There yet awaited me one more delightful day at the market. This time, not at the farm tables but set up in a tent on Pike Street itself. The market hosted the launch celebration of the fifth edition of my book *Joy with Honey*. What a day that was! My sister Marilyn came from Oregon to help me set it all up as well as James, my grandson. Friends from the YMCA water aerobics and friends from Maple Valley came, and the most fun of all was a surprise visit from cousin Mary Simon who flew in all the way from Pennsylvania.

Don was not there. He sat home alone with Catalina on his lap, watching the birds.

CHAPTER 19

Looking Ahead Through the Darkness

I cannot tell you when I realized that things were getting too much for us to handle. Don had always been a man very much in charge, like the old song goes: "I'll do it my way." It had to be *his* way—his orderliness, his radio stations, his music, or his need for silence. He was very strong-willed, vocal, and in charge. Determination is a good thing. You make a promise, and you are determined, come hell or high water, that you will keep that promise. Especially is this true when you make a promise to God, witnessed by over one hundred people at the altar on your wedding day: "I take this man as my wedded husband—for better or worse, for richer or poorer, in sickness and health till death do us part. So help me God."

I tell you now, there were times that I was tempted to call it quits. But the Lord gave me his very clear promise when I was but a child of age ten. He said, "I will be with you always. I'll never leave you or forsake you." I could sense his loving arms holding me so surely then that I have never, in seventy-five years, since forgotten it. I am so thankful that he is my good shepherd. He leads and he guides and he shows us the way—even through the dark days of dementia and Alzheimer's disease and even through embarrassment, humiliation, and abuse.

My dear reader, if Jesus can do this for me, he can do it for you too. He will guide you too. His still, small voice will give you songs in the night and "peace that passeth understanding." He did it for me.

It was a cold dark night just a few days before Christmas. I thought I heard a car coming up our long three-hundred-foot driveway. Don was half asleep in his La-Z-Boy with Catalina on his lap as usual. The only sounds were the crackling of the fire in the Glacier Bay woodstove. He was occasionally glancing at the *Birds and Blooms*, a magazine with beautiful, colorful pictures. He could enjoy that.

Suddenly, there was a soft knock on our door. I was delighted to see at least a dozen beautiful teenagers in our carport all decked out in scarves, stocking caps, and warm winter clothing. Here they were, ready for a night of Christmas caroling. I opened the door wide and began joyfully singing right along with them. I loved those kids. They were the cream of the crop—great young people from Peace Lutheran. A couple of them had been working with me at Pike Place Market on Saturdays.

But Don could not handle things out of the ordinary. Suddenly, he went into a fit of violent anger. "Get the hell off this property!" he screamed.

"Wait a minute," I said. "Please don't leave. This is my property as well. Just stay here for a couple of minutes. I've got an idea. I'll be right back."

I went back inside the house and dialed our dear neighbors, Ted and Gladys. I asked if they'd enjoy some Christmas carolers, and they said, "Yes. Great! We'll get out some Christmas cookies."

I joined them in joyfully singing all the happy songs of Christmas that night. My house was totally dark and locked up when I returned back up the hill.

Don was already sound asleep in bed. He never even mentioned the surprise nighttime carolers at breakfast the next morning. He was totally absorbed in watching the chickadees and downy woodpecker enjoying their suet just outside our dining room window.

He was in a fragile state of mind. We walked on eggshells trying not to rock the boat. He was trying to be in charge—captain of the ship, but that was far from reality. He no longer even remembered that once he had been a beekeeper. Memories of his childhood occasionally came up with amazing detail and clarity—especially when a friend or our daughter would come by for a visit. He enjoyed those visits. I think it was the high point of his week when Deena would drop in after her work to spend a little time with him.

I am so thankful to God that he willingly gave up his car keys and began letting me drive him around. One day earlier, after getting his haircut, he got lost finding his way back home. He eventually made it back but, in the process, racked up over one hundred miles on his Chevy S-10 pickup. I didn't question him too much. But I sure asked the Lord for guidance. He still liked getting into his truck and using it for little chores on the farm. He would drive around on our five acres and load up firewood he had been cutting and kindling, measured to precisely fit in the stove.

Another day, he had driven out to our meadow in his little pickup. He was determined to *do* something. The blackberry vines were growing across the roadway to our pump house. He took the long-handled clippers and began the strenuous job of clearing a path. I was not at home. When I returned, I saw the truck in the meadow and walked down to see what was going on. I found him on the ground, very confused and unable to get up on his feet. I didn't have my cell phone with me, or I would have called 911. I took a deep breath and breathed a silent prayer. Then remembering my sister's advice, I proceeded to help him very slowly and determinedly move his own body back up into the truck. She had learned from experience that it was next to impossible to lift a man off the ground. But she could help him by coaching where to move an arm or leg by encouraging him to muster all his strength to just do it. Somehow, Don was able, with my coaching, to crawl over to his truck and pull himself up into the driver's seat.

But sadly, he didn't know where he was. "What do I do now?" he said. "How do I get home? Where am I?"

"Look," I said, pointing toward our house and honey house barn. "Just drive across the meadow and up the driveway and you'll be home. I'll lead you around the big burn pile so you won't have to even back up. Follow me."

Miraculously, he was able to drive his truck back into the honey house and pull down the overhead door like he had easily done so many, many times in the past. It sat there for months after that day, until I finally convinced him that another beekeeper could get some good use out of it. We sold it to one happy beekeeper—Andy Matlitch.

After that, he stopped going into our honey house, and memories of beekeeping days began to fade. His world revolved around three square meals a day, a half hour of exercise on the stationary bike, Catalina, and watching the birds and wildlife on our five-acre wildlife refuge. It was very sad to me to see that not even a trace of memory was left of his former beekeeping days. This is what happens with dementia and eventually Alzheimer's. I knew I was not alone. Many others had struggled with their own loved ones going down that path.

"Dear Savior," I prayed, "please show me. Is there something I can do to help?"

The answer came. It came to me so clearly. Just like our Savior promised, "Ask and ye shall receive, seek and ye shall find, knock and the door shall be opened unto you" (Matthew 7:7).

A few days later, an idea popped into my head. I know it had to be from the Lord. I was prompted to get a photograph of him in his bee suit. I found a fun frame at our Maple Valley Bartell's, and I placed it on our dining room table, right in front of his place setting.

"What's that?" he said.

"Look, that's you, when you were a beekeeper," I replied.

The picture stayed there, right in front of him at the table for weeks on end.

Then one day when our very handy handyman, Bill Sloan, was having lunch with us, we were so surprised and happy to hear him say, "Hey, look at this. I used to be a beekeeper."

"Yes, you were!" said Bill. "And a very good one."

Oh, for the good old days. But reality told us that those days were but a memory. We were on a dark journey. But in the darkness, the Light of the world guided our way, not to see the end of the journey but one step at a time, one day at a time.

I will never forget the Friday evening after Thanksgiving in 2015. It was bitterly cold outside. Don was getting ready to go to bed, warming up a heating pad in the microwave and getting ready for bed doing his usual routine. I was quietly working on my Bible study fellowship lesson, sitting in Grandma's green rocker with my feet propped up on its matching footstool. I wasn't paying any attention to what Don was doing. He'd never had any difficulty getting himself to bed before. This night was different.

I heard him start the microwave, and the next thing I heard was his voice calling me, "We've got a problem here."

I bolted out of my chair and ran into the kitchen. There was a fire in the microwave, and it was still running, getting hotter and hotter. I automatically opened the microwave door to stop it, but when I did, flame and black smoke shot right out. I reached through the terrible smoke and slammed the door shut to contain the fire inside the microwave instead of catching the whole kitchen on fire.

Don went into the bedroom and closed the door. It was up to me to call for help. The smoke was too thick in the kitchen to even breathe. I went down in the basement and called 911. The smoke was also in the basement. It was hurting my lungs so bad. I ran outside in the frigid cold to wait for the fire department. The entire house was full of terrible smoke, and Don was inside. I called and called to him, but he did not answer me.

When the Maple Valley firemen came, the first thing they asked was "Is there anybody in the house?"

"Yes, my husband," I said.

They rushed in to get him through all that thick smoke, not even taking time to put their masks on. Don was confused and very difficult to deal with. They literally had to drag him out of the house. Once we were out, they had us both sit in my car out of the cold. But Don insisted on going back in the house in the smoke to find Catalina, his dear kitty. A fireman helped locate her under a shelf in the lowest place of the basement. Isn't it amazing the instincts that God gives to animals to survive? That black cat is still with me today—six years after the fire. In fact, she is sitting on my lap as I am writing.

Personally, my ordeal was not over. The smoke and hot flames had given me severe chest pain. I thought I might have even been having a heart attack. An ambulance whisked me right off to the Group Health urgent care in Bellevue and then sent me on over to the Overlake Hospital. I was having congestive heart failure. The Lord gave me his amazing "peace that passeth understanding." I received wonderful care and was so touched that my cardiologist, Dr. Rubenstein, came to check on me three times in the night. When I was released from the hospital a few days later, I was unable to return to our home because it still smelled so strongly of smoke. Our Grange insurance was in the process of doing a wonderful cleanup job for us, but even with a vaporizer, I could not be in the house. Very dear special friends, Mike and Priscilla McDevitt, graciously offered to let me stay with them while our home was being cleaned up.

Don insisted on staying in the house with Catalina during the whole long, drawn-out cleanup process. It was like he had to prove that he was the captain of a sinking ship and no one was going to make him budge. I was too sick myself to care for him. But I was at peace. I felt like I was being carried on eagle's wings.

It was especially at hard times like these that we were grateful for our daughter Deena Marie. She stepped right up to take care of her dad, cooking his meals and cleaning up in spite of the fact that she had a husband and two precious children at home. She also worked part-time in Seattle Children's Hospital. She was one very busy and efficient girl. What a blessing it is to have family. Our church family at Peace Lutheran was right there with us as well, prayer warriors, those who sent encouraging cards and those who brought meals on days that Deena was working. They were truly the body of Christ: putting love into action.

I was finally able to come back to my own home just a few days before Christmas. Don was happy about that. As I drove up our long driveway lined with pine trees and slowly circled around the back of the honey house, I was struck with the beauty of these five acres on which we had been blessed to live on for the past thirty-six years.

But at the same time, I very clearly heard God's still, small voice speaking to my spirit, "You need to get ready to move. I have a new home for you. You'll be telling these beautiful five acres goodbye."

"Yes, Lord, I hear your voice," I prayed. "You know I want to follow where you are leading. But where do I start? This three-thou-sand-square-foot honey house is loaded with stuff. Our house next door has accumulated way more than we need for a rainy day too. You know Don can't help me. Where do I even start?"

"Trust me," he said. "I will lead you one step at a time."

And you know, my dear reader, that is exactly just what he did. We should not be surprised though because this is exactly what God the Father Almighty promises he will do for his children. It's his very own promise to us in Psalm 32:8: "I will instruct thee and teach thee in the way which thou shalt go: I will guide thee with mine eye."

Don was not really unhappy when I began to purge and down-size because I kept reminding him that if something happened to us, we sure didn't want to leave Deena with all our mess. I gradu-ally began in the basement. Boxes and boxes of things went to the Goodwill, and more boxes of things went to our annual church yard sale to raise money for our youth and the National Youth Gathering. I also emptied the special closet I had designed in 1980 when our house was built. It was still full of clothing—now vintage—which I had made in my college days and later when I was teaching Bishop Method Sewing and Tailoring at Renton High School and Green River Community College. It's kind of strange now when I think about it. Things that once seemed so valuable in the past are now just a memory. Yes, memories of wearing them and memories of style shows and happy mother-daughter teas. But it was time to let go. I said yes. And I was peacefully led on.

"He leadeth me, oh, blessed thought. Oh, words with heavenly comfort fraught. What'er I do, where'er I be. Still 'tis God's hand that leadeth me."

I was making some noticeable progress in our house. It felt good to have things less stacked up and cluttered. And it was so nice to have all the walls and ceilings freshly painted.

In the meantime, things in the honey house just sat there, untouched. There were mountains of beekeeping paraphernalia—all the articles used for the past thirty-six years of activity related to bee-keeping. Don had not even stepped foot into his precious domain for the last couple of years. It was all up to me to clean out three thousand square feet of our bee barn.

Bill Sloan agreed to help me. He was a tremendous blessing, bringing me lots of long tables to start laying things out for sale. The word got out to the local beekeeping community that we were getting ready to have a sale. Several people came over early to get what they wanted.

I decided it would be fun to have a beekeeper's auction. I had never in all my life tried to organize and plan such an affair. But the Lord again miraculously guided me right down to the very last detail. I went to our Maple Valley Library and checked out a book on how to have an auction. That gave me a lot of good ideas. We set the date in April, when beekeepers were just thinking about new bees and more equipment in the spring. Bill helped me in organizing things. It was a humongous task.

A fellow I didn't even know volunteered to be the auctioneer. He told me he could play guitar and really put people in a happy mood while auctioneering at the same time. Wow, I thought, that might really be a lot of fun. I got all kinds of different duties lined up with wonderful friends who volunteered to help—everything from doormen to cashier, floor spotters, loader uppers, coffee servers, record keepers, and second pair to double-check, traffic directors, and guys to just stand around to talk about different beekeeping equipment to the novice beekeepers who might show up.

There were so many details to cover. About two weeks before our event, I was talking to Tina Robinson after church on Sunday.

"How's your auction plans going?" she said. "Do you have your bidding number cards made?"

"No," I said. "The book I checked out from the library didn't mention those."

"Well, you'll need them. I'll make some for you. Will one hundred be enough?" She did.

I had so much to learn. I was undoubtedly being led by my heavenly Father's hand. He sent people to help—for instance, the advertising.

I was shopping at Sunshine Corners and talking about our auction when Tony, the owner, said, "Hey, there is a guy in the store right now that you need to talk to. He'll get the word out to all the beekeepers. You can count on that! You came to just the right place at the right time."

And that is exactly what Andy Matlitch did for me. He notified the beekeeping clubs in Pierce County, Snohomish County, as well as King County. The word was out. I printed up a flyer.

A few days before the big day, I invited the key people who were lined up to help me come over for a roundtable discussion. We sat in a circle in the big open bay area of the honey house, surrounded by stacks and stacks of supers, bottom boards, covers, and every imaginable thing a beekeeper would ever need.

I began our planning meeting by first of all asking our volunteer musician auctioneer to tell us how he pictured the auction would run.

To the absolute shock of everyone in that circle, he said, "Well, I'm just gonna be there to play my guitar and put everybody in a good happy mood. I'm no auctioneer."

I could have fallen right off my chair. I couldn't believe what I was hearing. How could I have ever been so confused? *Now* what are we gonna do? The auction was only a couple of days away. But then, in my spirit, I was flooded with an inner calm and peace. And I remembered God's promise in Romans 8:28: "And we know that all things work together for good to them that love God, to them who are called according to His purpose."

"Don't worry, it will be okay," I said.

We went ahead and discussed the logistics of how we hoped everything would smoothly run. They all went home, and I went up into the house to fix dinner for Don. Suddenly, I remembered a beekeeper who had been by earlier a couple of times buying things a month or so ago. Hadn't he mentioned working in an auction house when he was young?

"I'm going to call Bob Bennett," I told Don. "Supper will be ready in half an hour. We need to find an auctioneer." I dialed his number.

He answered, and I explained our situation. He knew how auctions worked firsthand. Even though he had never been an actual auctioneer, he said, "Yes, I will do it for you." He did a wonderful job for us, and he also volunteered to bring his daughter to help out processing credit card sales. We were so blessed to have their help.

It was a successful auction with about sixty beekeepers in attendance. We made a good start in emptying out the honey house barn, and we were happy to pass on the supplies to other beekeepers. Everybody there was happy to see Don come down from the house for a very short time. It was the first time he had even been in the honey house for a couple of years. His very good friend, Dean Barnett, had come into the house and helped him navigate the walk down to a chair I had placed there, just in case. A lot of cameras were flashing. I wish I had a picture of that day. Maybe someone reading this will send me one.

We made a big dent in all the things in the honey house. But there were still a lot of things to clean up. We began planning to have another sale. This time, we'd have a barn sale and invite the general public. I gradually began bringing things down from the house to put out on the tables for sale—antiques; gardening supplies; books; Don's camping, mountain climbing, backpacking, and rock-climbing equipment; tennis rackets; and bowling balls. You name it. We were downsizing.

It was a tremendous amount of work getting ready for the big barn sale. Bill Sloan worked for weeks helping me get everything organized. Max and James spent hours on end getting all the cardboard boxes tossed down out of the loft and flattened for recycling. Jimm Butler, Jacob, Rachel, and Jimm's mother from Texas were there, helping to get ready for the sale.

I clearly remember the day we were almost ready to take a box of papers and stuff to the burn barrel when Jimm's mom said, "Wait, I think we need to look in that box."

She was right. We found Don's confirmation pictures from 1946. The box had been placed in the loft thirty-seven years ago. Finding that photo was so precious. It triggered a memory for Don of that most notable day when he confirmed his faith in the Lord Jesus. I placed it on the table beside the beekeeper photo as a reminder of his past.

I had also been scouting out different retirement homes in the greater Seattle area. I knew the best course of action for us was to follow the Savior's still, small voice. And he had told me clearly that it was time to move on. His faithful Word was my solid rock. "The eternal God is your refuge and underneath are the Everlasting Arms" (Deuteronomy 33:27).

About a year after the fire, there was another major disruption in our household. Totally unaware to us, our dishwasher was leaking. It had been leaking unknown for quite some time. One morning, I discovered that my clothes were wet on the shelf of the bedroom closet. On closer examination, I discovered that the wall and ceiling were damp with mold growing. It was no wonder that my allergies had been acting up on recent weeks.

Once again, I called our wonderful Grange Insurance people. They were pronto with all the fans and dehumidifiers. It was a noisy disruption so similar to what had happened a year ago with the cleanup after the smoke damage from the microwave fire. Things had just finally been all freshly painted, cleaned up, and put back in place; and now it was unbelievable we were being hit again. Bill Sloan had been our painter in 2015, and now we called him again to be our fix-it man for the downstairs closet which was just above the kitchen and dishwasher upstairs. Things seemed to be going pretty well on our cleanup project. The wet moldy drywall had been removed. The wet carpet was rolled back, and the fans and dehumidifiers were drying the inner walls. Upstairs, we knew we'd need new flooring in the kitchen and adjoining dining room. I actually had a nice light floor covering picked out.

We tried to avoid stressing out Don over this whole process. It was just too much for him to handle. Of course, he was not able to be at all involved in any of the decision-making. It was all up to me. The flooring contractors found a big problem when they started to work on our kitchen. They found asbestos. That meant a whole new crew had to come in and remove all the asbestos from the subflooring. They were a special hazard team. The whole work area had to be partitioned off with plastic sheeting, and the workers wore heavy-duty masks. But the bad news for us was really bad news—we had to get out of the house.

How in the world could I even begin to convince Don that we needed to pack up and go to a hotel for a couple of weeks? He was in such a fragile state of mind with worsening dementia. Anything that changed his usual, familiar routine would be a monumental feat to deal with. I dreaded even the thought of it.

But the Lord gave me an idea. Again, his faithful still, small voice spoke, "Tell Don about the toxic asbestos and tell him it's so dangerous it could kill his beloved Catalina."

"We need to get her out of the house while the workmen are here. We need to make a list of all the things she will need while she is away. Can you help me make a list? What will your cat need?"

Together, we made the list. I wrote it all down on a notepad:

dry cat food
canned cat food
kitty treats

litter box
litter scoop
extra litter
catnip toy
brush
cat carrier
her heating pad

"We do want to take good care of Catalina, right?" I said. "We don't want her to get sick from breathing asbestos."

He agreed.

Then a few hours later, I brought up the conversation again, getting down to the dreaded crucial point. "*We* have to get out of the house too. We are going to a hotel in Issaquah with Catalina. We get to stay in the Holiday Inn while the insurance company cleans up all the damage from the dishwasher leak and gets the asbestos out of our house. It's just as dangerous for us as it is for Catalina. So now we need to make a list for you too."

"I'm not going anywhere," he said.

But I kept trying to explain and have him help tell me what he wanted to take. We finally got our bags packed. And the next morning, a very nice social worker was at our door helping to get him into the car and then check into the Holiday Inn.

The Homewood Suites in Issaquah was a very nice, comfortable place to stay. A normal couple could have had a wonderful time there enjoying all the amenities. There was even a swimming pool, hot tub, exercise room, pool table, and a wonderful extensive breakfast bar.

But our stay was very far from a relaxing vacation. It was a nightmare with Don. There was nothing I could do to calm him down. That first night, he didn't have his comfortable recliner to sit in, and we had forgotten the Badger Balm that he always rubbed on his feet every evening before going to bed. He literally went *berserk*, screaming hours on end, violently agitated.

I was on the phone with everyone I could think of to try and get help. I even tried to locate a comfortable recliner for him to sit in. That was a dead end. There was none, even for rent, that I could locate. I was so worried that the hotel was going to throw us out for disturbing the peace. I had a pounding headache.

Somehow, the Lord helped me relax and get a few hours of sleep. I awakened very early the next morning and was prompted to leave and drive back to our house to get the foot balm before the workers got started on our house. Don was still sleeping. I wrote him a note and poured some granola in a bowl topped with sliced banana for his breakfast. I prayed a lot as I drove across the rural roads back to Maple Valley and back to the hotel.

When I returned a couple of hours later, he was watching television, content to sit in his wheelchair. That was just fine with me.

I was in no mood after last night's ordeal to stay in the hotel room with him all day. I told him I was going uptown to find the library. Maybe there would be a computer available where I could write our Christmas letter. Sure enough, there was, and there was also a nice librarian who gave me some coaching. In about half an hour, I wrote the following poem. It was amazing. God just gave me these words. He knew I needed a blessing. What a wonderful Savior we serve.

The repairs on our house took longer than planned. We were in that hotel room for close to three weeks. We both came out alive, and so did Catalina. Thanks be to God!

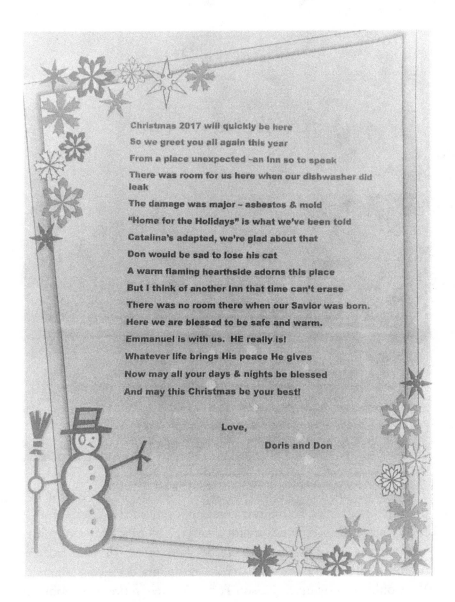

Christmas 2017 will quickly be here
So we greet you all again this year
From a place unexpected –an inn so to speak
There was room for us here when our dishwasher did leak
The damage was major – asbestos & mold
"Home for the Holidays" is what we've been told
Catalina's adapted, we're glad about that
Don would be sad to lose his cat
A warm flaming hearthside adorns this place
But I think of another inn that time can't erase
There was no room there when our Savior was born.
Here we are blessed to be safe and warm.
Emmanuel is with us. HE really is!
Whatever life brings His peace He gives
Now may all your days & nights be blessed
And may this Christmas be your best!

Love,

Doris and Don

CHAPTER 20

A Bittersweet End

$\mathcal{T}$he year 2018 was the last year of Don's life. It was a year of juxtaposition in our lives. So many events happened side by side. Through it all, I was truly given "beauty for ashes, the oil of joy for mourning, and the garment of praise for the spirit of heaviness" (Isaiah 61:3). As we turned the calendar to January 2018, the big decision was made. We would be moving to Judson Park—a lovely retirement home in Des Moines, Washington, not far from our family. Don could not comprehend what the future held. Alzheimer's disease had stripped him of cognitive reasoning.

A great number of wonderful friends and family rallied around me to pull off our big barn sale on a sunny Saturday in February. Bill Sloan had spent many hours and days—or was it weeks?—helping organize things in the honey house for this event. And to top it all off, he even surprised us by making stenciled T-shirts for all the people who helped out—young and older. They had a colored Mech Apiaries logo which Deena had designed several years earlier.

March came, and so did the first signs of early spring—swallows returning, swooping through the sky. In the meadow, golden dandelions bloomed with happy honeybees filling their pollen baskets. And in the woods, there were the bloom of Indian plum and wild cherry trees. I continued my task of being a full-time caregiver. My friends and family encouraged me to take a brief respite. This *was* a very difficult role to play for years on end. And how could I care for my husband if I myself were burned out or, worse, sick myself?

My friend, Linda, encouraged me to get a passport and join some other pilgrims from Peace Lutheran on a journey to Israel. So that is what I did. I boarded a jet plane and took the dream vacation of my entire lifetime. It was marvelous and inspiring beyond words. The Lord provided us with a sweet, efficient, dependable caregiver who I was able to hire for the two-week span of my absence. Somehow, Don accepted the fact that I needed to get away and was content with the caregiver coming in to meet his basic needs. I know this only happened because the Lord heard my prayers and the prayers of my fellow believing friends who were interceding to our Father in heaven. I returned, full of joy, new vigor, and determination to walk in the light, following my Savior. I had seen and walked where Jesus walked. I could never be the same again. Those memories were a new part of the very fibers of my being.

Then in April, I attempted to get us both moved into a nice apartment I had seen at Judson Park. Sadly, that did not work out. The idea of leaving our beautiful farm was too difficult for Don. Everything was put on hold. I was his full-time caregiver all throughout late spring and summer. I started taking him for long drives in the mountains, where he could enjoy the spectacular views of majestic peaks and tranquil forests. He seemed to enjoy those rides, but of course, he was unable to point out the names of all the mountains he had climbed long ago when he was with the Seattle Mountaineers. We celebrated our fifty-fifth wedding anniversary at Anthony's HomePort in Des Moines. He still enjoyed eating a good meal.

On August 10, we were blessed to host sixty friends and family at our Seventh Annual Harps in the Garden party. It was so very special. I knew it would be our last. Don wasn't interested in even showing his face.

On August 28, everything changed. He fell in the kitchen, breaking his hip and injuring his shoulder. He lived for just thirty-five days after that, in the hospital, then to a nursing home and rehab center, then to an adult family home, and then back to the hospital on palliative care. He was ushered into eternity as eight of us surrounded his bed singing, "I'll Fly Away," accompanied by Gail McEwen on her harp. God is good.

After his burial and memorial service, I moved on ahead contacting Judson Park again. The nice apartment I had fallen in love with earlier in the year of course was already sold to someone else. But there was another nice one, a bit smaller, awaiting just for me. I moved in the first week of November bringing, of course, Catalina, my prized dahlia tubers, all the honey I could store, and the furniture that Just Like Daughters recommended would fit in my new space. The moving truck pulled out and drove down our driveway. I was moving—moving from the five acres where sunrises were shown across the eastern skies and moving to the west where the western sky was shown with glowing sunsets overlooking the glorious waters of Puget Sound. Scenes began to unfold in my memory, foggy mornings where all we could see through the misty view from our dining room window was the faint outline of trees near the highway. Trees we had planted some thirty years ago as tiny saplings to block the sound of rushing cars speeding down the Maple Valley Highway. The beehives in the meadow were nearly invisible in the fog, but a black-tailed doe and its two fawns peacefully grazed on the green grass in the meadow and then meandered over to the French pussy willow, stretching up to nibble on the leaves. Such beauty. I paused, remembering the lovely rainbows spanning across the valley. Rainbows that were a reminder of God's faithful overshadowing love and his covenant, promises to us. And the eagles that soared above the Cedar River with their eagle eye on the lookout for a salmon below. There was a lump in my throat. There was also peace in my heart. I knew I was following my Savior's voice.

I picked up Catalina in her carrier and said, "Let's go, kitty. We are going to our new home."

But then suddenly I saw that we had a *big* problem. We had a flat tire. Now what? Things were packed to the hilt in the back of my Honda CR-V. I couldn't possibly even get to my spare tire, let alone change it. I was all alone now on five acres. At least I had my cell phone. I called Jimm Butler, who I had also agreed to be my realtor. Thankfully, he came to my rescue. But there was, of course, a notable delay in my arrival at Judson Park.

When I came into my new apartment at last, a joyous surprise awaited me. The Just Like Daughters girls already had all my furniture arranged and my bed made. As I walked in, they were putting dishes and linens in order in my new kitchen while two other girls were ready to hang pictures just where I wanted them. They were incredible. They even had all my books unpacked and artistically arranged on the bookcase shelves. I couldn't have been more pleased. But I was exhausted. Catalina and I just sat down and relaxed. I fixed a sandwich for dinner and went to bed early—never showing myself in public yet in the dining room.

The next morning, I still had things to unload out of the back of my car. I was fortunate to get a parking place in the garage right below my apartment. So all I had to do was walk a few steps to the elevator, and there was my car, parked safe and dry, out of the rain. I had several trips to make back and forth, getting things unloaded. My hands were full when I noticed two gentlemen getting out of their car.

"Hey, whatcha got there? Applesauce?" said the taller gentleman as he got out of the driver's side. He carried a Bible in his hands. "Are you moving in?"

Well, all my life I've been leary and cautious about talking to strange men, but these fellows must live here, and they were carrying Bibles. So it must be okay to have a conversation, I thought.

I walked on toward the elevator as we talked. "Yes, I'm just moving in. This big jar I'm carrying up to my apartment isn't applesauce. It's honey—a bit crystallized but perfectly good. It was made by our bees. So, of course, I'm bringing as much as I can fit in the cupboard. We used to have a honey business—a bee farm."

"Really?" he said, putting his hand on his temple to think. "I used to know a beekeeper who lived in Kent. Let me think. Oh yes, it was Mac West. Ever heard of him?"

Astonished, to say the least, I told him briefly the story of Mac, the newspaper article, and how he had been the very man responsible for giving Don the dream of making a career in beekeeping. Don had followed in Mac West's footsteps.

"Well, let me tell you," the tall older man said, "I was his pastor at the First Baptist Church in Kent. My wife, Betsy, and I knew him and his family too."

I was breathless. "This is amazing," I managed to say, still tightly holding the precious gallon of honey in my hands. I couldn't wait to get back up to my apartment—to sit down and take all this new information in, praying and thanking God for his amazing guidance. Out of at least seventy-five retirement homes in the greater Puget Sound area, I was right here in Judson Park exactly where God wanted me to be. I wish that Don would have known the final spin in the story of Mech Apiaries. The ending came full circle.

"Wait, we haven't made our introductions," the smiling tall man said. "My name is Paul Poehlman. And you?"

"Oh yes, my name is Doris Mech, of Mech Apiaries. Lots of people call me the Honey Lady."

"Well," he said, looking at his friend patiently standing near the elevator, "here is someone I'd like *you* to meet."

"This is Paul"—another Paul—"Paul Schumacher."

"I'm glad to meet you, Doris," he said as his warm hand tenderly clasped mine.

About the Author

Doris stems from Quaker heritage, growing up in a loving family of four in Oregon. She and her sister Marylin were surrounded by aunts, uncles, cousins, and grandparents on both sides of the family. She was privileged to earn her BA home economics degree at George Fox University. Going on, she taught high school in Moro Oregon, Selah Washington, Renton Washington, and Green River Community College.

She married Donald Mech, an electrical engineer at the Boeing company in 1963, never dreaming that ten years later they would launch into an unknown career with honeybees. Her first book, *Joy with Honey*, was published by Women's Aglow. Later, it was self-published in 1993. The second expanded edition was amazingly discovered by St. Martin's Press who brought it to the bookstores. The fourth and fifth expanded self-published editions are currently available to earnest seekers on the internet.

She currently resides on the outskirts of Seattle in a retirement community where, when not writing, she enjoys gardening, singing, walking, cooking with honey, and deepening friendships with family and special friends overlooking panoramic views of the Puget Sound.

Whatsoever thy hand findeth to do, do it
with thy might. (Ecclesiastes 9:10 KJV)